☀ INSIGHT COMPACT GUIDE

GUERNSEY

Compact Guide: Guernsey is the ideal quick-reference guide to Guernsey and the neighbouring islands of Herm, Sark and Alderney. It tells you all you need to know about the islands' attractions, from sand castles to real castles, impressive cliffs to quaint harbours, glorious gardens to pre-historic graves, and crafts workshops to a whole range of fascinating museums.

This is one of 130 Compact Guides produced by the editors of Insight Guides, whose books have set the standard for visual travel guides since 1970. Packed with information, arranged in easy-to-follow routes, and lavishly illustrated with photographs, this book not only steers you round Guernsey but also gives you fascinating insights into local life.

SA

D1479797

APA PUBLICATIONS L

Part of the Langenscheidt Publishing Group

Star Attractions

An instant reference to some of the top attractions of Guernsey and the other islands to help you set your priorities.

St Peter Port p18

Castle Cornet p19

Moulin Huet Bay p27

German Occupation Museum p28

Crafts workshops p32

Folk Museum p37

Le Déhus Dolmen p39

Boat trip to Herm p44

Sark's rugged coast p48

Seigneurie Gardens, Sark p51

Mannez Lighthouse, Alderney p58

Introduction

Guernsey – The Friendly Island 5
Historical Highlights 12

Places

Route 1: St Peter Port **18**
Route 2: Southern Guernsey **26**
Route 3: Central Guernsey **30**
Route 4: Northern Guernsey **35**
Recommended Walks on Guernsey **40**
Route 5: Herm **44**
Route 6: Sark **48**
Route 7: Alderney...**54**

Culture

Island Heritage **61**
Festivals **63**

Leisure

Food and Drink **65**
Active Pursuits **69**

Practical Information

Getting There **71**
Getting Around **71**
Facts for the Visitor...**73**
Guernsey for Children..**77**
Accommodation **78**

Index **80**

Guernsey – The Friendly Island

Opposite: boat ramp at Portelet

When Victor Hugo (1802–85) was sentenced to exile in 1851, he thought long and hard about where to make his new home. With the whole world to choose from, he nevertheless wanted to be as close as possible to his beloved France. Since he spoke only French, he wanted to live somewhere where French was understood. He dismissed Belgium because it had too little to offer by way of stimulus to his artistic temperament. He finally chose the Channel Islands because they were *'les morceaux de France tombés à la mer et ramassés par l'Angleterre'* ('morsels of France fallen into the sea and gathered up by England').

If Hugo felt perfectly at home in the Channel Islands, so did the islands' many other émigrés, including numerous British and Irish army officers and colonial servants who chose to settle here in the 19th century, retiring on generous half-pay. The effect they had was to dilute the Norman-French traditions of the islands, whilst adding new Anglian and Celtic ingredients to the existing mélange. The result is that today's visitors, who still come mainly from Britain, Ireland, France, Holland and Germany, encounter an interesting mix of cultures – part French, part English – which makes the islands feel reassuringly familiar, yet distinctively different.

Place names are both French and English

5

Similar but different

'Similar but different' is a phrase that could also describe the way the two main Bailiwicks of Jersey and Guernsey seek to differentiate themselves from each other. Though very alike in architecture, agriculture, geology and landscape, the people of each island work hard at creating subtle distinctions. Jersey and Guernsey have different currencies, phone cards and postage stamps, none of which are valid on the mainland or, except for currency, in the neighbouring island group. Letter boxes and post vans are different colours (red on Jersey, white and blue on Guernsey) and each claims its version of the classic knitted fisherman's jumper. Yet, while the word 'jersey' has entered the English language, the stylish Guernsey (which Nelson adopted as standard issue for the English navy) is far less well known, and the Alderney is a garment whose existence is known only to a few connoisseurs and knitwear historians (except in Australia, where the term is used for football shirts).

Letter boxes are blue

Guernsey people rarely refer to Jersey by name: to them, it is 'the other island'. They refer to inhabitants, only half in jest, as *crapauds* (toads) – because the toad is found on Jersey but not on Guernsey. Guernseymen, with their slower pace of life, are dismissed as *ânes* (donkeys) by their bigger-island rivals. Guernsey responds by calling itself 'the friendly island'.

Unspoilt landscapes
Empty bays

Location and size

As a group, the Channel Islands sit just off the Cherbourg peninsula (at its closest, the Breton coast is a mere 9 miles/ 14km away). Weymouth, the English coastal resort, lies some 80 miles (130km) due north, while the Breton port of St-Malo lies some 44 miles (70km) to the south.

With an area of 24 sq miles (62 sq km), and a population of 60,000, Guernsey is the second biggest of the Channel Islands after Jersey, but the more densely populated. It also has more cars per head of the population than anywhere else in the world – parking, especially in summer, can be a problem. The island is roughly triangular in shape, and divides into two quite distinct parts: to the south and east is the cliff-fringed 'high parish' region, where access to the beach is via deep wooded valleys or down steep rock-cut steps. The 'low parish' region to the north and west of the island consists of flat land fringed by miles of sandy dunes. The capital, St Peter Port (population 17,000), sits on the escarpment that marks the boundary between the highland and lowland zones.

Administration

The islands are divided into two Bailiwicks, each of which is governed by its own parliament. Self-government is a right that was granted to the islands by King John in 1204, as a reward for staying loyal to the English Crown after the rest of Normandy was conquered by King Philippe II of France. In practice, the islands delegate matters of foreign policy and defence to the UK parliament, but in all other affairs – especially in taxation and financial policy – they guard their independence zealously.

The southern Bailiwick of Jersey consists of Jersey itself, plus two groups of rocky islets that litter the Channel to the south, namely Ecréhous and the Minquiers Reef.

The northern Bailiwick of Guernsey consists of Guernsey, plus the islands of Herm, Jethou, Sark and Alderney, and a number of scattered lighthouse rocks and islets, such as Burhou, Ortac and the Casquests.

Herm

Tiny Herm lies just across the water from St Peter Port, a 20-minute ferry ride to the northeast. It is 1½ miles (2.5km) long by ¾ mile (1km) wide and has a population of around 50. The island is leased from the States of Guernsey and has been run as a family business since 1949. The new tenants, John and Julia Singer, have pledged to keep Herm as the 'jewel in the Bailiwick Crown'. The ban on cars and ghetto blasters continues, the White House (the only hotel on the island) will still be TV, clock and telephone free (although there's a phone for bookings) and seafood salads and crab sandwiches still prevail over burgers and chips.

The island is fairly flat, but has one magnetic attraction: the glorious Shell Beach, in the northeast of the island, composed largely of shells and shell fragments washed here by the Gulf Stream tides – a paradise for beachcombers.

Getting around Sark

Sark

Sark lies one step further to the southeast, reached from St Peter Port in 40 minutes by high-speed ferry. Prior to recent constitutional reforms the island was governed by the Seigneur in a system set up in the reign of Elizabeth I. The 450-year-old feudal state came to an end in 2008 when the Chief Pleas (legislative body) was reformed, Sark held its first general election and became Europe's newest democracy. The Seigneur still lives in the Seigneurie and now has a role akin to that of the Queen of England.

Sark is 3 miles (5km) long and 1 mile (1.5km) wide, with a population of 600. Consisting of a high flat-topped plateau, Sark is often described as two islands: Great and Little Sark are linked by a narrow natural causeway, with a 260-ft (80-m) drop to either side, called La Coupée (the Knife). This causeway, along with Seigneur's beautiful garden, is the island's major tourist attraction.

7

Alderney

Alderney is the northernmost of the Channel Islands, and the closest to France. Some 3½ miles (5.5km) in length, and 1½ miles (2.5km) wide, it is a roughly rectangular island, with a cliff-fringed plateau to the south and a northern half that slopes gently to a series of sandy bays.

Alderney's character differs somewhat from the other islands, partly because it was deliberately depopulated during the war, and used as a forced labour camp. There are Occupation-era fortifications all over the Channel Islands, but on Alderney they are particularly grim, scarring the island and evoking memories of suffering and death.

German battery on Alderney

Community life has been successfully rebuilt since the island's liberation in 1945, and Alderney is now a peaceful island once more, much visited by ornithologists and beach lovers looking for privacy and an escape from the busy world. It is also a centre for internet gambling.

Climate

Guernsey and the other islands are milder in winter and sunnier in summer than the rest of the British Isles, but strong winds can make temperatures feel cooler than they are. In the summer months the islands have a daily average of eight hours of sunshine and an average maximum temperature of 68°F (20°C). The best months to go are May to September, July and August being the hottest. The

Low tide at Pembroke Bay

St Peter Port prosperity

Atlantic sea temperatures are cool for swimming, averaging 62.8°F (17.1°C) in summer.

Tides

The islands have one of the largest tidal movements in the world and the coastal landscape undergoes dramatic changes between high and low water that almost doubles the size of the islands. Powerful tides roll back for miles, exposing huge areas of rock pools and clean, sandy and rarely crowded beaches. Fishermen forage along the foreshore for the lobsters, ormers, mussels, clams and oysters that end up being served as a *plateau de fruits de mer* in the island's many seafood restaurants.

Special status

Not surprisingly, given all their natural charms, the Channel Islands attract large numbers of visitors, and tourism underpins the little islands' economies, as well as being a major source of revenue for the bigger islands.

Visitors are attracted by the old-fashioned wholesomeness of the islands, but also by their VAT and duty-free status, which means that shopping for tobacco, booze and electronic goods is part of the Channel Island's experience (having said that, prices are not as cheap as shopkeepers would have you believe, and stores such as Marks & Spencer actually charge more for some lines because of the high costs of freighting goods to the islands).

Even after the abolition of duty-free allowances amongst EU members, the Channel Islands were not affected because of their special status: being neither part of the United Kingdom, nor of the European Union, they can set their own fiscal policy. Being small islands, they have no great need to raise large amounts of money from personal taxation. The almost complete absence of taxes on capital (no taxes on interest, capital gains, capital transfers or inherited wealth) makes the islands very attractive to wealthy incomers, and to the banking and investment community. On Guernsey as well as on Jersey, offshore finance has taken over from agriculture as the biggest employer, with many financial organisations using the islands as a base for trading in currencies, deposits, commodities, insurance and stocks and shares on world markets.

Going native

If you fall in love with Guernsey, and fancy spending your retirement years on the island, you had better be rich. A glance at estate agents' windows will reveal that there are two types of property on the market: reasonably priced accommodation and phenomenally expensive. One bungalow may be priced at £350,000, whilst its identical neighbour costs £1 million. The reason is that the cheaper bungalow can only be bought by a Guernsey native, whilst the millionaires' pad is for sale on the open market. By this means, Guernsey controls migration to the islands, which would otherwise be flooded by tax exiles. If you do succeed in becoming a resident, you will have to learn a new loyal toast. To the islanders, the reigning British monarch is still the Duke of Normandy and so, when they raise their glasses in honour of the monarch, they drink to 'The Queen, our Duke'.

Cows and carnations

Important as it is, the financial services industry is largely invisible to many visitors. Far more eye-catching are the green cow-filled fields of the inland valleys, or the glasshouses of Guernsey's flatlands. The cows, with the their doe eyes and dished faces, are a very special breed that has been selected since the mid-19th century. Hardy, but yielding large quantities of creamy fat-rich milk, the cattle on Guernsey were widely exported in the 1920s and 30s and are the genetic source of herds to be found in Australia, New Zealand and the Americas.

Once, mixed farming was the norm on the islands, and every farm had a cow or two. Now farms specialise, and large herds of cows are more normal, though you will still see cows tethered in the old-fashioned way, with a rope around their horns, grazing on L'Ancresse Common in the north of Guernsey.

High light levels, a gentle frost-free climate and long hours of sunshine provide excellent growing conditions on the islands, and the sandy, free-draining soil has been made fertile, over the centuries, by the liberal application of seaweed. In the mid-19th century, Guernsey was famous for its grapes, and many of the older houses in St Peter Port and around the island have ornate conservatories, known as vineries, as a legacy of this trade. The establishment of regular steamer services between the

9

Plenty to chew on

islands and Britain allowed more perishable fruits to be grown and sold. Until the 1980s, Guernsey toms – sweet, juicy and flavoursome – along with Jersey Royal potatoes and Evesham asparagus – were eagerly awaited by many people as early-season crops hinting of the tastes of summer to come. What was once a staple of English greengrocers' shops has now been driven out of the market by insipid Dutch imports, and Guernsey toms are virtually unavailable outside the island. Despite this serious economic blow, the ever resourceful horticulturists of Guernsey have instead turned their greenhouses over to cut-flower production and plant plugs, and the island supplies many of the freesias, roses and carnations sold in the UK. Horticulture forms the theme of several visitor attractions on Guernsey, and the island's natural profligacy is celebrated in its biggest festival, the Battle of the Flowers, which is held in August in Sausmarez Park.

Hedge stalls and the Clameur de Haro

If you are planning to wander Guernsey's lanes in summer, you probably do not need to worry too much about shopping in advance for picnic food. The chances are that you will be able to buy tomatoes, strawberries, fresh peas, apples, jam or chutney from one of the island's ubiquitous hedge stalls. Hedge stalls are an endearing feature of the islands, used for disposing of surplus garden produce – from cut flowers and the first of the season's new potatoes, to the inevitable giant marrows, courgettes and asparagus. Though the produce is usually placed in a wooden box by the gate, with a screw-top jar for your money, some enterprising stallholders will even wire up a fridge by the gatepost, selling homemade butter, cream and ice-cream. You may even find a stall selling home-baked Guernsey *gâche* (pronounced 'gosh'), a delicious tea bread made with butter and dried fruit.

Bucolic array and hedge-stall display

In the unlikely event that someone were to violate a green lane – by polluting the water, chopping down trees or bulldozing an ancient hedgebank – you might find yourself witnessing the island's famous Clameur de Haro. By this ancient custom, anyone who feels that their right to enjoy their property is being violated can effectively issue an immediate injunction by collecting two witnesses, kneeling before the offending party and declaiming: *'Haro, Haro à l'aide mon Prince! On me fait tort!'*. The catch is that you also have to follow this up by reciting the Lord's Prayer in Norman French. If you can do this, the other party must immediately stop whatever they are doing until the matter has been heard in the Royal Court.

Haro is probably Rollo, the Viking chieftain who became the first Duke of Normandy in the 10th century. Archaic as this custom may seem, it is taken seriously in Guernsey, and has been used to great effect: in 1830, it was used to prevent the demolition of Castle Cornet, and in more recent times, a St Peter Port newsagent used it against some demolition workers on a neighbouring site whose work was threatening his own property.

Flora and fauna

Inland, pretty high-banked lanes and tiny fields form a perfect landscape for wandering on foot or by bicycle. The banks and trees of Guernsey's green lanes provide valuable habitats for birds, mammals, insects and flowers. The Channel Islands were formed at the end of the last Ice Age, when rising sea levels, caused by melting glaciers, gradually flooded the land bridge linking the British Isles to the Continental mainland. Guernsey became an island some 2,000 years before Jersey, which left it with a slightly different flora and fauna – there are, for example, no moles or toads on Guernsey. On the other hand the island does have some species that are commoner on the Continent than in Britain: green lizards, for example, are relatively common, if shy, dune and wall dwellers on the island. Guernsey also has its very own bank vole, found nowhere else in the world.

Birdsong and butterflies accompany any walk, and the islands are colourful with flowers, from the yellow and blue of spring primroses and violets, to the bluebells in May and the purples of massed thrift, campion, foxglove and orchids in June and July. The sheer quantity of colour, on clifftops, road verges and in wooded valleys, creates a strong visual impact and shows what we have lost elsewhere through too lavish use of herbicides.

The coastal fringes have their own distinctive wildlife, from the puffins and gannets that nest on the offshore islets, to the sea kale, horned poppy and sea holly that grows on the dunes and shingle banks. Fishermen regularly bring home spider crabs, lobsters, oysters and mussels, but catching ormers is now strictly regulated, since over-fishing threatens to wipe out the remaining population.

The ormer, or sea ear, was once a staple of the Channel Islanders' diet, and somewhat disdained because of the effort involved in cooking this oyster-like mollusc, which only becomes tender and edible after simmering for many hours. Related to the abalone, much loved by Chinese gourmets, it is found beneath rocks in the island's tidal sandbanks, and has a distinctive shell, well camouflaged from the outside with its sand-coloured exterior, but beautifully iridescent inside with its pearly rainbow sheen. The ormer gathering season now lasts from January to the end of April (on the lowest tides), and the best of the diminishing stock usually ends up on the menu of one of the islands' first-class hotels (such as the Côbo Bay Hotel – see page 78). The taste, if you can afford it, has been compared by some to mushrooms, by others to chicken.

Agapanthus

11

Lobster pots and ormer shells

10,000BC Guernsey becomes an island when it is cut off from the mainland of France by rising sea levels at the end of the Ice Age.

8,000BC Stone-age nomadic hunter-gatherers migrate to Guernsey and become the island's first settlers. Flint and bone tools from this period have been excavated from Castle Rock and are displayed in the Castle Cornet Maritime Museum.

4,500BC Construction of Les Fouillages (located on Guernsey's L'Ancresse Common Golf Course), the oldest of the many passage graves (or dolmens) to be found on the island. These massive communal graves, constructed of granite boulders under an earthen mound, indicate that the rulers of the island during this period command considerable resources and manpower.

2,250–70BC Finds of socketed axes and fine jewellery indicate that the islands engage in maritime trade during the Bronze and Iron Ages. Also from this period is the carved menhir, Gran'mère de Chimquière, the figure of a fertility goddess.

3rd century AD Evidence of continuing trade between Guernsey and the Continent comes from a Gallo-Roman boat, excavated recently in St Peter Port, and now displayed in Castle Cornet's Maritime Museum. Pitch, pottery, quern stones, glass, bronze and coins are among the ship's cargo. St Peter Port itself lies on top of a substantial Roman settlement, and there are the remains of a fort on Alderney, at the so-called Nunnery, facing out onto Longis Bay.

AD556 St Sampson brings Christianity to Guernsey, creating a church looking to Brittany for its leadership and character. Parishes are established, named after hermits and saints who found small monastic cells on the island.

565 St Magloire, nephew of St Sampson, establishes a monastery on Sark.

933 William Longsword, the 2nd Duke of Normandy, annexes the Channel Islands, which become part of the Duchy of Normandy.

1066 William the Conqueror, the 10th Duke of Normandy, conquers England and establishes the first constitutional links between Britain and the Channel Islands.

1204 King John loses his French lands, except the Channel Islands, to King Philippe II. The English defeat left the Channel Islanders with a stark choice: to maintain their allegiance to Normandy, or to side with England. They chose the latter, which was probably the most significant event in the island's history as the islands are rewarded with considerable independence, which continues until today.

1250 Work on Castle Cornet begins. Chateaux des Marais and de Rocquaine strengthened to defend the harbour and west coast from the French.

1338 The French capture Jersey and hold it for seven years in one of many skirmishes between France and England disrupting life on Guernsey.

1484 An Act of Neutrality is granted by the Pope to the people of the Channel Islands, so that their ships are free, in theory, to sail unmolested, even during times when England is at war.

1564 With Queen Elizabeth I's approval, Sark is colonised by Helier de Cartaret, who divides the island into 40 parcels of land and grants a perpetual tenancy to the occupants in return for help in defending the island against pirates using Sark as a base from which to attack English ships.

1560s Trade in wool between Southampton and the Channel Islands leads to the rapid growth of the knitwear industry, with the islands exporting high-quality sweaters, stockings and gloves to England and France. So profitable is the trade that local laws are passed to ensure that essential agricultural work is not neglected.

1589 Paul Ivy, one of Europe's most innovative military architects, supervises the construction of Castle Cornet, Guernsey's main fortification, guarding the entrance to St Peter Port harbour.

1642 Sir Peter Osborne, Lieutenant and Governor of Guernsey, refuses to surrender Castle Cornet to the Parliamentarians during the English Civil War. Held under siege until December 1651, Castle Cornet becomes the last Royalist stronghold in the British Isles to surrender.

Early 18th century Guernsey entrepreneurs establish the Newfoundland trade, catching cod in the fishing grounds of Newfoundland and trading the salted fish for cargoes of spice, timber and sugar in the Caribbean which they carry to Spain and trade for wine and citrus fruits.

Mid-18th century Privateering, whereby Guernsey ships are licensed to capture enemy shipping and confiscate their cargoes, becomes a major source of revenue for the island. As England imposes duty on imported luxury goods as a means of funding its wars with France, Spain and the American Colonies, Guernsey, ironically, becomes a major supplier in the smuggling trade, shipping large quantities of captured brandy, perfume and lace to southern England.

1770s Methodism gains a strong foothold in the Channel Islands following the visit of John Wesley to Alderney and Guernsey, replacing the older Huguenot-influenced Calvinism.

1780s Guernsey's 15 coastal towers are built, along with Fort George, to defend the islands against attack from the soldiers of revolutionary France.

1782 Construction of St Peter Port's market halls.

Late 18th century Guernsey becomes a supply post for British troops fighting in Spain and Portugal during the Napoleonic Wars. The stationing of soldiers here brings prosperity to Guernsey but begins the erosion of the islands' ancient Norman language and traditions.

1813 Publication of the first English-language newspaper on Guernsey.

1836 Silver is discovered on Sark, but the mines are worked out by 1847 and abandoned.

1847 Construction work begins on the breakwater on Alderney, designed to create a secret base for the English navy, conveniently close to France.

1840s Granite begins to be quarried on Alderney, Sark and Herm in great quantities, and shipped to England for use in construction.

1900 English becomes the official language of the States, the island parliament.

1920 The novelist Compton Mackenzie leases Herm and Jethou.

1923 Guernsey adopts sterling currency in place of the French franc.

1939 Guernsey Airport opens, just a few months before the outbreak of the World War II.

1940–45 The Channel Islands are occupied by the Germans, who build substantial fortifications.

1944 The population of Guernsey is saved from starvation when the Red Cross ship, the *Vega*, reaches the islands just before Christmas.

1945 The German forces occupying the Channel Islands surrender unconditionally on 9 May.

1949 Peter Wood, the first Tenant of Herm, takes on a 100-year lease of the island, and begins to transform it from a bramble-choked wilderness into today's island paradise.

1950s Tourism booms as UK visitors are curious to see the aftermath of German occupation.

1977 Last sailing of a non-car ferry. First finds from a Roman wreck in St Peter Port harbour.

1981 Guernsey's oldest tomb is discovered at Les Fouaillages.

1985 New Guernsey flag flown for first time.

1992 Elizabethan ship discovered off Alderney.

1994 Guernsey buys Lihou Island.

1999 Sark modifies its inheritance laws to comply with European human rights requirements.

2004 The islands celebrate 800 years of the special relationship with the English Crown.

2008 The lease of Herm Island is transferred to John Singer; he and his wife take over as island managers from the Heyworth and Wood families who had overseen Herm since 1949. In December Sark sees its first general election.

2009 In Sark the new democratic Chief Pleas (legislative body) is sworn in after 450 years of feudalism.

ROUTES 2-4
GUERNSEY

0   1   2   3 km
0   1   2 miles

N

Saline Bay
Côbo Bay
Rocque de Guet
Côbo
Fort Hommet
Albecq
Vazon Bay
Câtel
Lihou Island
Le Trépied Dolmen
Perelle Bay
Richmond
Le Gelé
Fort Saumarez
St Apolline
Kings Mills
Les Anguillières Nature Reserve
Perelle
Mont Saint
Le Creux ès Fales
L'Erée
Frie Baton
St Saviour Reservoir
L'Erée Bay
St Peter in the Wood
St Saviour
Les Lohiers
Rocquaine Bay
St Saviour's Tunnel (closed to the public)
Les Buttes
Guernsey Clockmakers
Les Arquets
Coach House Gallery
Longfrie Inn
Guernsey Woodcarvers
Le Gron
La Villiaze
Fort Pezeries
Fort Grey Shipwreck Museum
Les Reveaux
Les Bréhauts
Bruce Russell & Son
Guernsey Airport
Table des Pions
Portelet Harbour
Guernsey Pearl
Silbe Nature Reserve
St Peter's Church
Les Nouettes
Le Bourg
Pleinmont
Torteval (detached)
Les Sages
Torteval Church
Torteval
Les Landes
German Occupation Museum
Pleinmont Point
Pleinmont Observation Tower
St Peter (detached)
Torteval
Les Villets
Forest
Belle Elizabeth
Bon Repos Harbour
Corbière Bay
Pointe de la Moye

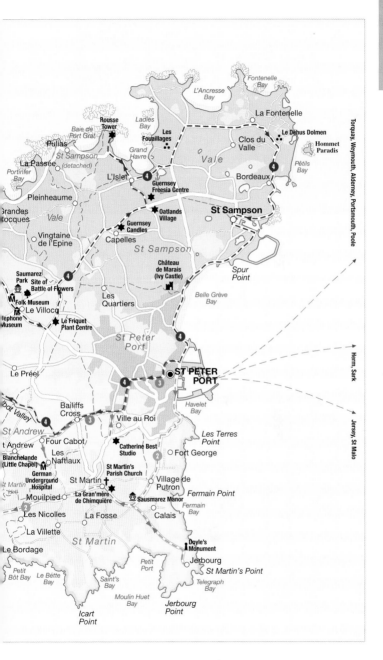

Torquay, Weymouth, Alderney, Portsmouth, Poole

Herm, Sark

Jersey, St Malo

Fontenelle Bay

L'Ancresse Bay

La Fontenelle

Rousse Tower

Ladies Bay

Baie de Port Grat

Les Fouaillages

Clos du Valle

Le Déhus Dolmen

Hommet Paradis

Pulias

St Sampson (detached)

Grand Havre

Vale

Pêtils Bay

La Passée

Portinfer Bay

L'Islet

Bordeaux

Guernsey Freesia Centre

St Sampson

Pleinheaume

Grandes Rocques

Vale

Oatlands Village

St Sampson

Vingtaine de l'Epine

Guernsey Candles

Capelles

Les Quartiers

Spur Point

Saumarez Park

Site of Battle of Flowers

Château de Marais (Ivy Castle)

Belle Grève Bay

Folk Museum

Le Villocq

Telephone Museum

Le Friquet Plant Centre

St Peter Port

Le Préel

ST PETER PORT

Havelet Bay

Bailiffs Cross

Ville au Roi

Les Terres Point

St Andrew

Four Cabot

bot Valley

St Andrew

Les Naftiaux

Catherine Best Studio

Fort George

Blanchelande (Little Chapel)

German Underground Hospital

St Martin

St Martin's Parish Church

Village de Putron

Fermain Point

St Martin Ticket

Mouilpied

La Gran'mère de Chimquière

Sausmarez Manor

Fermain Bay

Les Nicolles

La Fosse

Calais

La Villette

St Martin

Le Bordage

Doyle's Monument

Petit Bôt Bay

Le Bette Bay

Petit Port

Jerbourg

St Martin's Point

Saint's Bay

Telegraph Bay

Moulin Huet Bay

Jerbourg Point

Icart Point

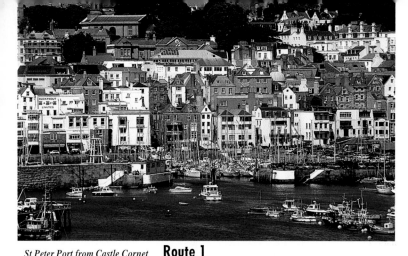

St Peter Port from Castle Cornet

Route 1

Preceding pages: return to harbour

Note: the dialling code from the UK for Guernsey and the other islands in this book is 01481. From outside the UK, dial 44-1481.

St Peter Port *See map on page 20*

St Peter Port is a very attractive place, with a bustling port, backed by a town that rises very steeply from the sea, so that the buildings appear piled on top of one another. They are certainly stratified socially, with the seafront Esplanades lined by tall and unadorned warehouses, most now converted to shops, pubs and restaurants, and the grander houses of 18th-century merchants on the hilltop above. These, too, have undergone conversion – some of the fine houses along Grange Road and The Queen's Road now belong to wealthy banks and financial services organisations, but their conversion to offices has been carried out with sympathy for the original buildings.

As a result, St Peter Port has some of Britain's best-preserved late-Georgian and Regency architecture – less grand than Cheltenham or Tunbridge Wells, but impressive in its sheer variety.

Guernsey Information Centre
Yachts in the harbour

Along the waterfront

A good place to begin exploring the town is the excellent **Guernsey Information Centre ❶** (tel: 01481 713888; Mon–Fri 9am–6pm, Sat 9am–1pm; also Sat pm and Sun am in summer), on North Esplanade, with its informative displays and helpful staff. The centre is housed in a building of 1911 whose grey granite makes it look rather austere – perhaps deliberately so, as this was once Guernsey's administrative centre, where all the departments needed to run the island were based. The information centre sits on land that was reclaimed at the beginning of the 20th century. Originally, ships docked right alongside the warehouses that line the right-hand side of **Quay-**

side, allowing cargoes of wine, citrus fruits, spices, sugar and wool to be lifted straight from the ship's hold into the tall Dutch-style warehouses, whose large loading doors have been replaced by windows. Most are four or five storeys tall, with one set of shops on the lower two floors, entered from Quayside, and another set of shops on the upper floors entered from the High Street, which runs parallel to Quayside but higher up the hill. Linking Quayside and the High Street are a number of steep lanes, called *venelles* (Guernsey-French dialect for 'little passages'). Look up as you explore them – some are roofed over using massive timbers from broken-up ships.

On the opposite side of Quayside is the **harbour**, with its mixture of sleek yachts, workaday fishing boats, cargo ships and inter-island ferries. Booths along the embankment sell tickets for ferries to Herm – departures for Sark, mainland Britain and France go from St Julian's Pier, over to the northern end of the Esplanade.

Heading south, you will come to St Peter Port's busiest road junction, overlooked by a **statue of Prince Albert**, erected to commemorate a visit made by Victoria and Albert in 1846. Opposite is the **Town Church**, considerably restored in the 19th century, but incorporating the nave of the town's earlier medieval church. Restoration was necessary because the church had much of its original fabric damaged during the Civil War. One of the war's ironies was that the town, and the castle that was intended to protect it, were on opposite sides in the war. St Peter Port sided with the Parliamentarians, whilst the governor of Guernsey, naturally enough, supported the Royalist cause and successfully survived a nine-year siege from his base in Castle Cornet. The Royalists bombarded the town with such success that shipping was forced to move to St Sampson's harbour, further up the coast (still the site of Guernsey's main commercial port).

Castle Cornet was then accessible only by boat – today's visitors explore the castle by walking out along Castle Pier, (which, along with the lighthouse at the end, was built in 1866), from where optimistic anglers cast out their lines. ★★★ **Castle Cornet** ❷ (tel: 01481 721657; www.museum.guernsey.net for all attractions; Apr–Oct daily 10am–5pm) is a delightful maze of buildings and courtyards, linked by steps and passageways, with little gardens tucked into sheltered corners. There's a daily **noon-day gun ceremony**, when an 18th-century cannon is loaded and fired. Several buildings within the grounds have been converted to museums, so allow plenty of time to see everything. At 2pm on most days during the summer Living History performers present a series of stories about life in the Castle and St Peter Port from Tudor times to the German Occupation.

Prince Albert

19

Castle Cornet and gunners

The Story of Castle Cornet, housed in the Lower Barracks, traces 700 years of turbulent history. The **Royal Guernsey Militia Museum**, in the 18th-century hospital buildings, includes the tragic story of the death of the Royal Guernsey Light Infantry in spring 1917. The **201 Squadron Museum** covers 'Guernsey's Own' air heroes.

Castle Cornet has four period gardens reflecting domestic life during the 16th to 18th centuries. There are guided tours at 2pm on most Sundays in the summer.

The oldest part of the castle survives only in fragmentary form – the original keep and most of the medieval

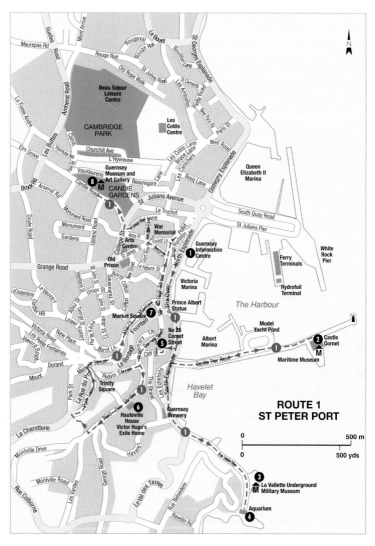

ROUTE 1
ST PETER PORT

buildings were destroyed when the castle magazine was struck by lightning on 29 December 1672, killing the governor's wife and mother, and five other people. Displays show the results of archaeological excavation to recover the form of the original medieval castle, while the present fortress is substantially Tudor in date. It was the first English-built castle to incorporate ideas borrowed from Italy – thicker masonry to absorb cannon fire, as few vertical faces as possible (oblique and rounded faces were better at deflecting cannon balls) and bastions projecting at intervals along the curtain wall to provide gun platforms and protect the walls from direct attack.

Garrison life in the castle
An impregnable stronghold

The success of this design was proved by the Civil War siege, when the castle proved all but impregnable, and again when, during World War II, the Germans occupied the castle and found it necessary to make very few modifications to fit it for modern warfare.

Two other museums within the grounds are housed in the 18th-century barracks. The **Maritime Museum** looks at the relationship between St Peter Port and the sea from Roman times through to today's high-speed catamarans. The exhibits include some very well-preserved pottery from medieval wrecks and material from the Roman galley found in St Peter Port. On the floor above, and only open for specific events, is the **Hatton Gallery**, full of portraits of governors and merchants, dramatic seascapes and some fine views of St Peter Port.

In July and August there is a season of outdoor theatre in the Castle grounds, ranging from Shakespeare's *Comedy of Errors* to *Ali Baba and the 40 Thieves*. In bad weather plays take place in the art gallery.

Guernsey Brewery

Continuing along the Esplanade, you will pass the bus terminus and the **Guernsey Brewery**, on the right, with the town's main bathing beach to your left (sandy at low tide) before coming to the green end of St Peter Port, where gardens and trees cloak the steep hill above the undercliff footpath. Continue along here for a short way and you will soon reach ★★ **La Vallette Underground Military Museum ❸** (tel: 01481 722300; mid-Mar–mid-Nov daily 10am–5pm). The simple concrete-lined opening in the cliff leads into a complex of tunnels built by slave labourers during the Occupation. The tunnels served as a refuelling station for U-boats, and one of the huge fuel oil storage tanks has survived. The exhibition, like so many concerned with the war, consists of a mass of largely unexplained materials, with few labels, though the occasional letter, document or newspaper cutting offers clues as to their significance.

It is remarkable that some objects have survived at all: the museum starts with a display of Red Cross food parcels delivered by the Swedish ship, the *Vega*, towards the end

Operations room at La Valette

of the war, when the population of the Channel Islands was starving. To people used to surviving on a meagre diet of seaweed jelly, bramble-leaf tea and parsnip-root coffee, the food parcels, filled with milk, cheese, butter, chocolate, tinned salmon, raisins, dried egg, oatmeal and peas, would have come as much-needed relief.

Right next to these displays, relating to the final difficult months of the war, are posters detailing arrangements for the evacuation of the islands in 1940, when it was clear that the Germans intended to invade. What was not clear, as the posters show, was whether or not the British government intended to send an evacuation ship to take off those islanders who wished to leave. In the end, 9,000 people – over half the islands' population – managed to escape in fishing boats and cargo steamers, including almost the entire population of Alderney.

Another exhibit reminds us that most of the islands' fortifications were constructed by forced labour – whips and rubber truncheons bring home the brutal nature of the Channel Islands' regime. The people of the Channel Islands themselves were protected to a degree from exploitation by the Hague Convention, which the Germans observed, stating that local people could not be forced to construct works of military character, especially against their own country. Even so, there were reprisals against the civilian population, including the confiscation of radio sets and execution for acts of so-called espionage. Others were interned in Biberach Camp, in Bavaria, from September 1942 until May 1945, and there are some moving exhibits of Christmas gifts and cards made by the internees and sent back to their families.

From the Underground Military Museum, the South Esplanade continues a short way to another tunnel: this one was built in 1861, as part of a scheme, never completed, for driving a road through to Fermain Bay *(see page 26)*. The Germans constructed several side tunnels, using Russian labourers who left their hammer and sickle symbol on the rocky roof.

Tropical fish at the Aquarium

Today the tunnels house the ★★ **Aquarium** ❹ (tel: 01481 723301; daily 10am–dusk), displaying examples of the many and varied fish to be found in Guernsey's waters – from perfectly camouflaged baby soles and the tiny inhabitants of tidal pools, to larger conger eels and dogfish. There are also prettily patterned tropical fish, with notes on their habitats, and their suitability for use in home aquariums, a collection of reptiles in a vivarium and a new terrapin island.

To the High Town

Returning to Castle Pier, the causeway that leads out to Castle Cornet, climb up the steep lanes on the left that lead

right past the Yacht Inn, then left to the prettily cobbled intersection of four different alleys, then right up Coupée Lane. You should come out alongside ★★ **No 26, Cornet Street ❺**, a remarkable building that serves as the headquarters of the National Trust of Guernsey. The offices lie behind the well-restored 18th-century shop and parlour, where costumed shopkeepers sell toys and souvenirs (8 Apr–mid-Oct Tues–Sat 10am–4pm).

Hauteville: the view from St Barnabas

Turn left out of the shop, and you will pass, on the right, the former church of St Barnabas the home of the Island's Archives, from whose car park there is a superb view over the red-tiled rooftops of Guernsey. Further on, Tower Steps, with its pubs and restaurants, has a pleasing group of late Georgian and Regency buildings and beyond, on the right, lies Pedvin Street, with its long curving terrace of late Georgian houses.

Hauteville houses

Continue left here into **Hauteville**, where the increasingly large and ornamented houses give some indication of the status and wealth of the people who first settled here when the area began to be developed in the 1780s.

The street's most famous resident was Victor Hugo, who lived from 1856–70 at ★★★ **Hauteville House ❻** (tel: 01481 721911; guided tours by appointment only, in English or French, Apr–Sept Mon–Sat). The house has been preserved as it was and the gardens brought back to their original splendour. Hugo was more than a little eccentric, and the house is a physical manifestation of his quirky ideas about monarchy, history and patriarchy.

Hauteville House, Victor Hugo's exile home

Having been thrown out of France, branded as a dangerous radical for his opposition to the *coup d'état* staged by Prince Louis Napoléon in 1851, Hugo first settled in Jersey, where he kept up a tirade of invective against '*Napoléon le petit*' as he styled the French Emperor, through his newspaper, *L'Homme*. In the same paper, he criticised Queen Victoria for making a state visit to Paris

Novelist Victor Hugo

in 1855. This so angered the people of Jersey that Hugo was expelled once again – this time moving a short distance north to the island of Guernsey. Here he installed his wife *(Madame, la mère de mes enfants)* and family at Hauteville House, and Juliette Drouet, his mistress *(Madame, mon amie)* at No 44 Hauteville, a short way up the road.

Whilst living here he wrote some of his best-selling novels, including *Les Misérables*. Growing wealthy for the first time, he indulged his taste for woodworking and interior decoration. Thanks to the anti-Church zeal and anarchy of the Napoleonic period, churches throughout Europe had been gutted of woodwork and paintings, and antiques dealers had huge stocks of Renaissance and medieval carving for sale.

Hugo bought chests and pews and broke them up to line the walls and ceilings of his rooms, adding his own embellishments, to create a house that is dark, brooding and full of symbolic meaning. Significantly, he chose to write his powerfully romantic novels in a room that was, by contrast with the rest of the house, flooded with light – he constructed a rooftop observatory of glass, with far-reaching views over the blue seas to his beloved France.

The Old Market and High Street shopping

From Hugo's house, turn left and explore Hauteville, turning right down Park Lane Steps, and then right again to reach Trinity Square. This attractive corner of St Peter Port has several good restaurants and a number of antique shops – especially in cobbled and pedestrianised Mansell Street, which leads back to the centre of town, emerging at the **Market Square** ❼. Having undergone major renovation the old market is now more of a shopping mall and, in summer, a venue for open-air musical and theatrical performances. Some traders, however, still sell fish and flowers at the north end.

Even if you aren't all that keen on shopping, it is worth exploring the maze of shop-lined alleys, called the Arcades, to the left as you emerge from Market Street, along with the High Street and its extension, Le Pollet and Lower Pollet. Many of the shops along these streets have attractive Regency, Victorian and Edwardian shop fronts – and there are several cafés along the route where you can stop for coffee or cakes or relax alfresco.

Along the High Street

Civic St Peter Port

At the junction of High Street and Le Pollet, Smith Street leads left and uphill towards the **Royal Court House**, centre of island government and administration. Walking up Smith Street, do not miss the lace-like cast-iron detailing of the ironwork decorating the facade of Marks

& Spencer's clothing shop. Also along this street you will find several good bookshops, selling a comprehensive range of books on Channel Islands history.

At the top of the hill, to the left, is the appropriately sombre court house, in which the States of Deliberation, which governs the Bailiwick of Guernsey, held its first meetings in 1803. In the same building are the island's courts – civil and criminal. They are located only a short step away from Guernsey's main police station, which occupies the former workhouse, La Maison de Charité. To find it, turn round and go back past the little garden at the top of Smith Street, then head straight across, down Hirzel Street. This will bring you to the gates of the former workhouse. On the gatehouse is a plaque showing a pelican pecking her breast to feed her young with her own blood, the traditional symbol of charitable self-sacrifice, and the 1742 date stone.

Royal Court House detail

Turn left here and walk up Hospital Lane to emerge by the **War Memorial** on St Julian's Avenue. Cross over to Candie Road and the entrance to peaceful, flower-filled **Candie Gardens**. The gardens (along with the building that now houses the Guernsey Museum) was bequeathed to the islanders in 1871 and turned into a public park. A pretty French-style bandstand, standing alongside the house, was recently converted into an excellent café.

The ★★★ **Guernsey Museum and Art Gallery 8** (www.museum.guernsey.net; daily 10am–4pm, May–Sept until 5pm) is built around a collection left to the States of Guernsey by Thomas Guille and Frederick Allès, who emigrated to New York and became partners in an interior decorating business. As they prospered, they poured their wealth into books about the Channel Islands, which they eventually bequeathed, along with fine porcelain and antiquities, weapons and furniture. In addition, the Lukis Collection consists of finds excavated from local megaliths and tombs by an amateur archaeologist. These are joined by informative exhibits on the geology, wildlife, and history of Guernsey and the smaller islands.

Candie Gardens

Exhibits in the adjacent art gallery include Rodin's bust of Victor Hugo (1883), wearing a most expressive frown and wild beard, and Renoir's painting of *Fog on Guernsey* (also 1883). There are also characterful sketches by Peter de Lievre (1812–78) of island farmers and fisherfolk.

Incorporated within the museum is a Victorian cast-iron bandstand from where the Café Victoria offers fine views across to the islands. The surrounding **Candie Gardens** (Apr–Oct 10am–5pm, Nov–Dec and Feb–Mar 10am–4pm, closed Jan), home to a statue of Victor Hugo, have recently been restored. Brass bands strike up here on Sunday afternoons in summer.

Victor Hugo at Candie Gardens

Route 2

Southern Guernsey

St Peter Port – Fermain Bay – Sausmarez Manor – Jerbourg Point – St Martin's Village – German Occupation Museum – Pleinmont Peninsula – Fort Grey – St Peter Port *See map on pages 16–17*

Fermain Bay

Sausmarez Manor

Stalking the grounds

To explore southern Guernsey, leave St Peter Port along the South Esplanade, passing Castle Cornet and bearing right by the Guernsey Brewery to follow the main road uphill. The road twists and turns from here up a delightful wooded valley, bright with bluebells in spring, to emerge on the grassy common that fronts the entrance to Fort George, the massive garrison that was built to protect St Peter Port at the turn of the 18th century. Turn left to follow Fort Road, and you will pass the Fermain Valley Hotel, at the head of the road leading down to ★★ **Fermain Bay**. There is no vehicular access to the pretty bay so your best bet is to continue down to Jerbourg Point, park by the Doyle Monument, and walk along the cliff path.

If you do this, you will first pass the entrance to ★★★ **Sausmarez Manor**. Take a tour of the house (Apr–Oct daily 10.30 and 11.30am, June–Sept additional tours at 2pm) and you will discover that this is the stronghold of one of Guernsey's oldest families: the de Sausmarez family have lived here since 1254, and a fine series of family portraits hangs in the imposing grey granite house, which dates from 1714. Delightfully informal gardens surround the house, where you might possibly trip over free-range ducks and hens scrabbling for food in the undergrowth as you explore the lake and extensive woodlands. There is a nine-hole **pitch-and-putt course** (daily 10am–5pm) alongside the manor, the **Copper, Tin and Silversmiths' Workshop** (daily 10am–5pm) and, set in and around the subtropical woodland, formal gardens and a couple of small lakes the ★ **Art Park** and sculpture trail. One of the first and most varied sculpture parks in Britain, it shows around 220 works by 90 artists.

Beyond the manor, the left turn leads down to Jerbourg Point. At the first of two car parks on the peninsula you can stop and climb to the base of the ★ **Doyle Monument**, commemorating Sir John Doyle, Lieutenant-Governor of Guernsey from 1803 to 1816, for sweeping views along Guernsey's eastern coast. Further south, the second car park commands views over the rocks of ★ **St Martin's Point**, and southwards towards Jersey.

Back on the main road, the first left turn will take you down a pretty green lane to the ex-Moulin Huet Pottery

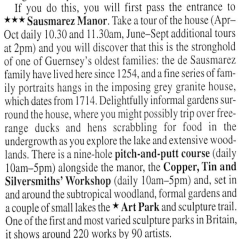

(closed indefinitely). From here, there is a pleasant walk down the leafy valley road to ★ **Moulin Huet Bay**, with its sea caves and a waterfall cascading down the cliffs. The painter Pierre-Auguste Renoir, who stayed in St Peter Port during the late summer of 1883, was so inspired by Moulin Huet that he made 15 sketches of the picturesque cove.

Where the main road meets **St Martin's Village**, there is a cluster of shops and banks. It is worth parking here and walking up the narrow green lane that leads northwards to visit St Martin's parish church and pay your respects to the ★★ **Gran'mère de Chimquière**. This Grandma is considerably older than most and, though stony faced, she nevertheless flaunts her naked breasts for all the world to admire. She is, in fact, a 4,500-year-old mother goddess carved in granite, standing at the entrance to St Martin's churchyard and, if you visit after a wedding, she is quite likely to be wearing a garland of flowers: newly weds traditionally place flowers on her head for luck and fertility. Grandma was carved at two separate stages during her long life: around 2,500BC the block of granite was erected here, dressed and smoothed to create a female figure with breasts, folded arms and a girdle. During late Roman times, around AD200 or 300, the facial features were recarved, and Grandma was given a set of curls and a short buttoned cape falling around her upper torso.

From St Martin's, follow signs to the airport along Guernsey's south coast road. To the left, after a mile, some of the island's most attractive water lanes run down to ★ **Petit Bôt Bay**, a popular bathing spot and one of the

Gran'mère de Chimquière

Moulin Huet Bay

Petit Bôt Bay

German Occupation Museum: 'V' For victory

Wartime kitchen in the museum

Torteval church

island's sunniest and most sheltered bays. The brooks that run down the side of these lush green lanes used to power two mills, one of which was used for paper making.

Just before the airport entrance, a left turn leads to Forest church and the ★★★ **German Occupation Museum** (Apr–Oct 10am–5pm, restricted opening hours off season). This is one of the Channel Islands' better war museums, with some interesting and unusual items displayed amongst the general mass of weapons, ration books, uniforms and medals. At the entrance, for example, there are wartime photographs taken by German soldiers, in which they are cooking rabbit stew in a cauldron and looking just like Boy Scouts on a camp. A large painting depicts a Rhine Valley scene, complete with castle and vineyards, painted on the walls of a nearby house by a homesick soldier. Another rarity is a stone painted with a red V (for Victory) sign. Guernsey people showed their defiance by painting such signs wherever they could until the occupying troops took to painting laurel wreaths underneath to represent German victory.

There are wartime condoms (German issue) and a doll's house made from cardboard boxes, and letters from the Controlling Committee of the States of Guernsey giving instructions for the distribution of food and the slaughtering of pigs during the dark days towards the end of the war when food was desperately short. Surprisingly, cigarettes did not need to be rationed – experiments in growing tobacco on Guernsey proved very successful, ensuring an unlimited supply of locally made cigarettes.

The museum's reconstruction of a wartime kitchen on Guernsey brings home just how little the islanders, and the occupying troops, had to live on, once the Allied landings in Normandy had cut off vital supply lines from the Continent. Surviving on a diet of bramble-leaf tea, acorn coffee, marrow pudding and potato bread, the only variety in the diet came from the occasional jelly made from carrageen moss (a type of seaweed) served with sugar beet syrup. There is also a reconstruction of a Guernsey street, with shops and people, as it looked in 1940, and there are videos to watch explaining the various types of German fortification to be seen around the island.

To see one of the most striking of these fortifications, continue past the airport, and take the left turn opposite Mon Plaisir House. Follow this road to the tip of the Pleinmont peninsula (passing Torteval church on the right, with its unusual round tower and witches'-hat spire), where you can park and explore the coastline at this southwestern tip of Guernsey. **Pleinmont Observation Tower** (Apr–Oct Wed and Sun only 2–5pm) is a prominent and unmissable feature on this windy headland, a five-storey concrete tower, pierced by viewing slots. It was from here that German observers controlled Guernsey's coastal artillery, communicating instructions to the gunners by radio so that they knew where to direct their fire.

On the same headland is the ★ **Table des Pions**, a grassy mound encircled by a ditch. This played a prominent role in a medieval ceremony, the Chevauchée de St Michel, when officers of the feudal court inspected the highways and sea defences to ensure that local landowners were fulfilling their duty to maintain them. The pions were the footmen who accompanied the officers and the Table des Pions was the spot where they took a break to enjoy an open-air banquet. The Chevauchée (briefly revived in 1995) was banned in 1837 because the pions, following what they claimed as an ancient right to kiss any women whose path they crossed, made free with the governor's wife.

Table des Pions

Returning up Guernsey's western coast, there is a sheltered sandy beach at **Portelet Harbour**, a good spot for a swim if the tide is out. Beyond is a pretty wooded valley, owned by the National Trust of Guernsey, after which the main road heads up to ★★★ **Fort Grey** (Apr–Oct daily 10am–5pm), housing a shipwreck museum. In summer (Tues–Sat) there are living history presentations in which a militiaman recounts tales of derring-do.

Named after the governor of the day, Fort Grey was built in 1804 as part of a Sir John Doyle's grand scheme for defending Guernsey against potential attack from Napoleon's army. With its outer curtain wall, and inner tower, the fort is aptly known as the Cup and Saucer. The museum in the tower is largely concerned with the many wrecks that litter Guernsey's western shores, including the notorious Hanois reef. Building a lighthouse on the reef in 1862 reduced the annual toll of ships, and in 1975 the shipping lane for ocean-going vessels was moved 10 miles west to avoid further casualties. On display are many items taken from wrecks, including the cutlery, fine candlesticks and coffee pots from *SS Yorouba*, which foundered in 1888.

Fort Grey

29

For refreshments, try ★ **Guernsey Pearl** (specialising in local cultured pearls), with a café serving snacks and lunches, opposite Fort Grey. To the north of the fort, ★ **Rocquaine Bay** merges with ★ **L'Erée Bay**, at low tide, to form one continuous stretch of sand – Guernsey's biggest beach, with safe swimming, rockpools to explore and beachside toilets.

Inland, bird lovers should seek out the ★ **Silbe Nature Reserve** in the Rue du Quanteraine. Though it consists of little more than a group of fields watered by a stream in the Quanteraine Valley, it attracts plenty of birds and is a pleasant spot for a stroll.

Guernsey Pearl

Route 3

German Underground Military Hospital – Little Chapel – Bird Gardens – Creux ès Faies dolmen – Fort Saumarez – Lihou Island – Le Trépied – St Apolline's Chapel – St Saviour's Tunnels *See map on pages 16–17*

Elizabeth College
Grange Road

Traffic passing through St Peter Port is channelled along the Esplanade, then out of town along St Julian's Avenue and up to College Street, passing **St James's** church on the left. The church was built in 1818 and converted to become the island's principal concert and arts venue. It was recently extended to include new galleries, a café and in the basement, in a special gallery to house Guernsey's most successful Millennium Project, a tapestry that took four years to make and shows scenes depicting 1,000 years of island life. Opposite St James is a new court complex.

Opposite is the neo-Gothic bulk of **Elizabeth College**, founded as a school in the 16th century and rebuilt in the 1820s using the proceeds from a special tax of a shilling on every gallon of spirits sold in the island.

Ahead lies **Grange Road**, with some fine 18th- and early 19th-century villas and terraces, many now converted to bank premises or guest houses. The houses of this period on the Channel Islands have nearly all retained their ironwork around the front garden and area steps, unlike mainland Britain, where much architectural ironwork was removed during World War II and turned into munitions.

Turn left at the next junction and you will see the even grander houses that line **The Queen's Road** (originally known as La Petite Marché, but renamed when Queen Victoria visited Guernsey in 1846). All are set in spacious park-like gardens, including Government House, with its sentry boxes at the gate, which was acquired by the States as the residence of the island's governor after World War I.

Catherine Best

At the next set of traffic lights, a slight detour will take you to see the Catherine Best jewellery workshop. Turn left, following signs to the airport, and straight on at the next junction, with its petrol station and supermarket. The second turning left, shortly after the junction, leads to a converted windmill where **Catherine Best**, one of the island's most creative jewellers, has her ★ **workshop and showroom** (Mon–Sat 9am–5pm, May–Oct also Sun 10am–4pm).

Returning to the traffic lights, turn left and continue for just under a mile, until you pass a left turn, signposted

to the ★★**German Underground Military Hospital**
(Mar and Nov Sun and Thur 2–3pm, Apr and Oct daily
2–4pm, May, June and Sept daily 10am–noon and 2–4pm;
July–Aug daily 10am–noon and 2–4.30pm).

Tucked away inconspicuously down a green rural
lane, this is one of the largest complexes in the Channel Islands constructed during the Occupation era. The
hospital is a testimony to Hitler's mistaken belief that
the Allies would, as a matter of pride, eventually seek
to attack and retake the Channel Islands. Hitler entrusted
the task of fortifying the islands to Dr Fritz Todt, who
had earlier been responsible for planning and building
Germany's *autobahn* system. Organisation Todt, as it
came to be known, involved turned the Channel Islands
into an impregnable fortress, with artillery able to cover
a whole sweep of the French coast, from Cherbourg to
Cap Frehel.

This hospital, along with its counterpart in Jersey, was
intended for the treatment of German military casualties
in the event of an attack. Built underground, the wards and
operating theatres were hewn out of solid rock by slave
workers from Russia, Poland, Alsace and the Czech Re-
public, many of whom died as a result of the brutal treatment meted out by the German Occupying Forces. In the
event, the hospital was never used for the purpose for
which it was built – instead, it was employed principally
as a store for the vast quantities of munitions stock-piled
by the Germans.

31

From this dank and chilly spot, go back to the main road,
follow the sharp bend to the left and then take the first
right turn to reach the ★★**Little Chapel** (accessible
all year). This charming building *(see picture on page
60)* is a complete church in miniature, claimed to be

*Keeping time at the Clockmakers
German Underground
Military Hospital*

Guernsey Bird Gardens

the smallest church in the world. Begun in 1923 by Brother Deodat of the De la Salle Brothers, owners of the adjoining school and estate, the chapel is 16ft (5m) in length and is encrusted in shells, coloured pebbles and china fragments.

Nearby at Les Vauxbelets, just a few minutes' walk away, is ★ **Guernsey Clockmakers and Martyn Guille Silversmiths** (tel: 01481 236360; Mon–Fri 8.30am–5.30pm, Sat 10am–4pm), where you can watch the silver craftsmen and study the intricate workings of the grandfather clocks, watches and barometers being made or repaired in this craft workshop.

Returning to the crossroad, turn left and you will come to the workshop of ★ **Guernsey Woodcarvers** (tel: 01481 265373; daily 10am–5pm), where craftsmen work on a variety of projects involving the restoration of antique furniture or the creation of new items, from lathe-turned bowls and lamps to cabinets, cupboards and music stands.

Back on the main road, turn right and you will shortly come to another establishment where craftsmen work while you watch and, if you wish, ask questions. Here the staff of ★ ★ ★ **Bruce Russell & Son** (tel: 01481 264321; www.bruce-russell.com; Mon–Fri 10am–5pm, with demonstrations at 10.45am) make beautiful objects from gold and silver, including candlesticks, goblets, napkin rings and spoons, caskets and the famous Guernsey milk can and loving cup. The family business of goldsmiths, silversmiths and jewellers has been going since 1887. Award-winning Bruce has received commissions to design pieces for presentations to celebrities, heads of state, the Vatican and the British royal family. The complex has a well-regarded restaurant and is set in an 8-acre (3-hectare) garden and nature reserve.

Bruce Russell & Son

The road from here wriggles round the western end of the airport and joins the main road; turn right here to continue west, past the Longfrie Inn (excellent if you have children, with an indoor Fun Factory play area) and the ★ **Coach House Gallery** (daily 10am–5pm) exhibiting the work of local artists, with a pottery workshop and etching studio alongside.

Coach House Gallery

At the next junction, turn left and park in the car park on the left-hand side of the road to explore the headland at the northern tip of L'Erée Bay. The first site of note, just up from the car park, is the ★ **Creux ès Faies** dolmen. The name means 'Entrance to Fairyland' and, with a little imagination, it is not difficult to see why it got this name. The tomb is surrounded by a granite wall of alternate vertical and horizontal stones, and you can crawl into the dark interior to look up at the two massive stones capping the

whole structure. The prehistoric passage grave was probably built around 3000BC and continued in use for 1,000 years or more, with successive burials and cremations being placed in the chambers, along with gifts of pottery, flint and stone tools.

Just beyond the dolmen, going uphill, there is a pretty tea garden, where good-value sandwiches, salads, cream teas and home-baked cakes can be enjoyed (Tues–Sun in the high season, 10.30am–5pm). High on the headland above is ★ **Fort Saumarez**, which has the appearance of a World War II artillery control tower. In fact the wartime structure was constructed on top of an older Martello Tower, built in 1805.

Continue downhill from the tower and you will come to another car park with a large monument commemorating those who lost their lives when **MV** *Prosperity* foundered on the reefs off Perelle Bay in January 1974 with the loss of all 16 crew. From the car park, a path leads down to the causeway linking mainland Guernsey to the island of ★★ **Lihou**, which is now a nature reserve, noted for its seabirds and wildflowers. This tranquil haven was purchased by the States of Guernsey in 1995. A notice at the head of the causeway gives the times when it may safely be crossed (the tide returns very swiftly, and can cut you off). If you are planning a trip you can also find the times of the tides in the *Guernsey Evening Press*. Apart from its wildlife, the treeless island is mainly of interest for the remains of the 12th-century priory of **Notre Dame de Lihou**, of which little now remains except a few wall fragments and a rock pool, known as Venus' Pool, large enough to bathe in.

Another nature reserve, this time consisting of a shingle bank, stands to the east of the Fort Saumarez Head-

Creux ès Faies dolmen

33

Fort Saumarez

Looking across to Lihou

Le Trépied dolmen

St Apolline's Chapel

St Saviour's Reservoir

land, running alongside the main coastal road. Yellow horned poppies grow on the landward side of this bank, called **Les Anguillières**, and sea kale grows on the seaward side. The fields on the opposite side of the road served as Guernsey's first airport and alongside there is an area of wet meadows and ponds where snipe, kingfishers, wagtails and warblers can be seen.

Continuing round the headland, stop in the next car park at the southern end of Perelle Bay, and cross the road to find the dolmen called ★ **Le Trépied**. This prehistoric passage grave was reputed, according to the amusing sign alongside, to be the place where local witches met with the devil for Friday-night revelries.

At the next junction, turn right (inland) and follow the road around the sharp left-hand bend. Soon afterwards, stop to admire ★★ **St Apolline's Chapel** (open daylight hours). The granite chapel, built in 1394, is a single cell building and thought to be the only remaining medieval chantry chapel in Guernsey. It has wall paintings that are believed to show the *Last Supper* and the *Betrayal*. The chapel had been used as a cowshed before the States of Guernsey bought it in 1873 and rescued it from this humble role. The site was sympathetically restored in the 1970s as a Chapel of Unity. The work included underfloor heating and the reconstruction of a bell tower, but because of continuing problems with damp more conservation work is taking place. It is open to the public free of charge and an inter-denominational service is held each Thursday morning.

Continuing inland, take the second main turning right (signposted to St Saviour's) to follow a delightful winding road up past **St Saviour's Reservoir** to the hilltop parish church. Hikers will appreciate the pleasant 2-mile (1.5-km) walk that was laid out around the reservoir as a millennium project. The large and impressive church is medieval in origin, and was partly rebuilt in 1658 after the spire was struck by lightning. A stone path to the west of the church leads downhill to the pretty stream which feeds the grounds of the Auberge du Val *(see Leisure, page 66)*, a rural guest house with a popular restaurant, whose herb and vegetable garden is occasionally open to the public.

Turning left here will bring you to the entrance to **St Saviour's Tunnels** (closed to the public for safety reasons), a massive complex built during the World War II Occupation, that burrows right beneath St Saviour's church. The Germans chose this site for their main ammunition store on the reasoning that the RAF would be very unlikely to bomb a church, or even suspect what lay beneath the churchyard.

Route 4

Côbo Bay

Northern Guernsey

St Peter Port – Talbot Valley – Vazon Bay – Côbo Bay – Saumarez Park – Folk Museum – Le Friquet – Le Grand Havre and Ladies' Bay – L'Ancresse Common – St Peter Port *See map on pages 16–17*

Flat Northern Guernsey has an entirely different character from the southern and central uplands. Fringed by sandy beaches, the west-facing coast is backed by dunes and sandy common, too poor to farm, but now used as a public golf course. There are plenty of opportunities for bathing so be sure to bring swimming costumes and towels if you are heading this way. Inland, the region is more heavily developed, with industrial complexes around St Sampson's and numerous greenhouses producing cut flowers.

A day at the seaside

The area also has many small reservoirs, most of them worked-out quarries now used for water storage (others serve as refuse tips, fish farms, car parks or industrial sites). These northern quarries produced roadstone, kerb stones and paving setts for export to the British mainland. They also supplied the grey diorite from which the older houses of the north are built, as well as many Napoleonic-era towers and fortifications that line the northern coast.

It is the whitewashed stucco of Regency terraces that we see first, however, heading out of St Peter Port along Grange Road and The Queen's Road *(see page 30)*, followed by pink granite farmhouses as we head west past Princess Elizabeth Hospital. Turn right at the next major junction to drive down the green ★★ **Talbot Valley**. Part of the way down this steep-sided valley, grazed by sandy-

Brooklands Farm Implements Museum

The gun at Fort Hommet

Saumarez Park's Folk Museum

brown Guernsey cows, you will pass Guernsey's only working watermill on the left. This is one of six mills in the valley, surviving in various states of repair.

Further down on the right is a car park in an abandoned quarry and a footpath (the **Ron Short Walk**, named after a past chairman of the Guernsey National Trust) which climbs the valley side and affords good views over an undeveloped, peaceful and green part of Guernsey.

At the bottom of the valley **King's Mills** is named after three watermills that once stood on this ancient site, drawing on the power of the Talbot Valley stream. From here take the next major left turn to descend to sandy ★★ **Vazon Bay**, deservedly one of Guernsey's most popular beaches. This is the sports playground of the island, with surfers and sandracers, and shore fishermen bringing in bass and mullet. A special area is designated for surfers, and if you want to join in, the recently established Guernsey surf school offers coaching for all abilities and hires out wet suits, kayaks, surf- and bodyboards.

★★ **Fort Hommet**, a solidly built Martello tower of red granite stands on the headland to the north of the bay. Wherever you find Napoleonic fortifications, there are sure to be German defences in the vicinity, for the Occupation troops appreciated the skills of their predecessors in finding sites from where artillery could cover a large sweep of coast. Here, a German gun casemate (Tues, Thur and Sat 2–5pm) has been restored and, unusually, it retains its original 10.5cm gun.

Continuing round the coast, you next come to ★★ **Côbo Bay**, another fine bathing beach, and the home of a well-established windsurfing school. You can join the locals and visitors who sit outside the **Côbo Bay Hotel** to watch the windsurfers or for a fine view of the sun setting over the sea. Côbo Bay is backed by a worked-out quarry and, if you climb the steps to the top of the now-wooded quarry, you will find the **Rocque de Guet Watchhouse and Battery**, a Napoleonic watchtower, from where there are some fine views of the western coast.

From Côbo Bay turn inland along the main road that bisects the village. After about half a mile (1km), at the next crossroads, turn left, and you will find on the left the entrance to ★★ **Saumarez Park** (open daylight hours and not to be confused with Sausmarez Manor in St Martin). Children are in their element here, with a big adventure playground located alongside the car park, and excellent tea rooms.

Saumarez Park and the imposing French-style house at its southern edge were created in the 18th century by William Le Marchant before coming, through marriage, into the hands of the de Saumarez family, and once stood at the centre of a large and wealthy estate. The entire property was purchased in 1938 by the States of Guernsey, and opened to the public.

The ★ **house**, now the Hostel of St John, is used as a residential home for the elderly. Formal gardens surround the house, very much in the same French idiom as the house itself. Both reflect the tastes of St James Vincent de Saumarez, the fourth Lord Saumarez, who spent much of his life as a diplomat in the British Embassy in Paris. Laid out in the 1880s, the gardens are planned around a central axis, with three fountains, and sombre clipped evergreens. Less formal are the shrubberies, planted with the camellias and bamboos that Lord Saumarez saw during diplomatic visits to Japan.

Saumarez House

To the rear of the house, beyond the tearoom, is the National Trust of Guernsey's newly restored ★★★ **Folk Museum** (24 Mar–mid-Oct daily 10am–5pm). This excellent museum is housed in 18th-century farm buildings grouped around a courtyard. The first part contains a series of reconstructed rooms showing a typical cottage kitchen of 100 years ago, and the drawing room of a middle-class home, with costumes and furnishings of the period. There is also a display of Victorian seaside clothing, plus grander gowns, fans and purses worn as evening wear.

Dolls at the Folk Museum

Upstairs, a display on childhood contrasts the comfortable life of the nursery with the harsh working life of many children, put to work in granite quarries or trimming and pruning greenhouse fruits, from an early age. Clever children could escape hard labour by becoming clerks and wrestling with such knotty problems as: a merchant in Paris remits to his correspondent in London 400 crowns; at 4s 6d each. What is the value in sterling?

Implements in the outbuildings

The outbuildings now display a whole variety of tools and implements used in domestic and working life in Guernsey at the turn of the century. Crab pots and fish baskets, rabbit traps and pig-killing knives, milk cans and threshing tools all give an insight into the varied diet and the never-ending round of work involved in rural life before mechanisation.

Turn right at the exit from Saumarez Park, then left at the road junction, and you will soon arrive at the ★★ **Guernsey Telephone Museum** (tel: 01481 257904; May–Aug Wed–Thur 2–4.30pm, occasional openings in Apr and Sept). Manned by Friends of Guernsey Heritage, this free museum is more interesting than it sounds, with telephones and switchboards tracing the development of telecommunications on the island from 1896. Children will have fun playing with the old-fashioned phones, most of which are still in working order. Turning left from the

They're all candles

Oatlands Craft Centre

Guernsey Freesia Centre

museum and taking the next major left turn brings you to **Le Friquet Plant Centre and Café** (daily all year round from 10am).

This is just one of a cluster of attractions in the vicinity that are ideal for rainy days. Turning right from Le Friquet, and right at the next junction, you will pass three further attractions. ★ **Guernsey Candles** (tel: 01481 249686; daily 9am–5.30pm) has candles in every conceivable shape and size as well as displays on making your own.

At the next junction, the right turn will take you to ★ ★ **Oatlands Village** (daily 9.30am–5pm) where gift shops and craft workshops are grouped around a courtyard set in a converted brickworks, complete with bottle-shaped kilns. Attractions here include a model railway exhibition and shop, a doll's house collection and a children's play area.

At the same crossroads, the left turn takes you to the ★ **Guernsey Freesia Centre** (tel: 01481 248185; daily 10am– 5pm), where you can see (and smell) freesias at different stages in their growth. A video detailing the history of the island's cut-flower industry conveys some very impressive statistics, such as the fact that Guernsey exports 40 million roses to mainland Britain every year – apparently the high light levels enjoyed by the island encourage the growth of long straight stems – perfect for cut flowers of all kinds.

Due north of the Freesia Centre is the sheltered and sandy beach at **Le Grand Havre**, separated by an area of seaweed-covered rocks from the equally attractive **Ladies' Bay**. While you are here, you can visit the ★ **Rousse Tower** (daily from 9am), which stands on the headland to the west of Le Grand Havre. One of a chain of 15 towers built in the 1780s against the threat of invasion by France, it has been fully restored and contains displays on the history of Napoleonic-era fortifications on Guernsey.

From the high points on **L'Ancresse Common** at the very northern end of the island, you can see many such fortifications. Here the horizon bristles with tall circular towers and square forts, spaced at regular intervals, each one guarding a possible landing site and intended as a show of strength to deter Napoleon from planning an invasion. Far harder to see is the oldest prehistoric site on Guernsey, hidden among the gorse and bracken on the southern edge of the common. Named ★ **Les Fouaillages**, this roofless burial chamber, consisting of a ring of fallen stones, was constructed more than 7,000 years ago and discovered as recently as 1977.

Sandy Pembroke and Lancresse Bays provide the last opportunities for bathing as the island's northern road

Le Déhus Dolmen

fringes the common and turns south: from here on, the beaches are rocky and subject to fast currents. Just after the road turns south, look for a narrow lane on the left which leads to ★★ **Le Déhus Dolmen** (open all hours), Guernsey's most atmospheric passage grave. Not only is the dolmen perfectly preserved, with a small wooden door for an entrance, it is also furnished with an electric light. Turning on this light dramatically throws into relief a mysterious carving on the underside of one of the tomb's massive capstones. This shows the figure of a bearded man, armed with bow and arrows, known as the Guardian of Le Déhus. Some scholars have suggested that the figure had already been carved on the stone before it was incorporated into the tomb, in which case it would predate the construction of the dolmen, which is itself more than 4,000 years old.

39

Continuing south, you will see the tall tower of **Vale Mill** (1850) high on a hillock over to the right as you skirt the fishing port at Bordeaux Harbour and head for the busy commercial port at **St Sampson's Harbour**, with its shipyards, power station, oil tankers and coal docks. Though not the island's most attractive town, St Sampson nevertheless attracts visitors for its many duty-free outlets, ranged along the harbour front.

St Sampson's Ivy Castle

As a last stop, before returning to St Peter Port, look out for the Château de Marais standing on the fringes of a housing estate inland from Belle Grève Bay. Known locally as the ★ **Ivy Castle** (open daylight hours) it is no longer ruined and ivy clad, but has been well restored to illustrate a sequence of defences, from the earliest 13th-century moated bailey, to the 18th-century powder magazine and the inevitable concrete bunker, built when the Germans re-fortified the castle during World War II.

Start at the steps

*Havelet Bay and Castle Cornet
from Fort George*

Recommended Walks on Guernsey

Walk 1: St Peter Port to Fermain Bay

Fermain Bay, with its sheltered Mediterranean ambience, is one of Guernsey's most picturesque spots, but it is rarely crowded because the only vehicular access is by a private road, closed to all but permit holders, and there is no nearby parking. The best way to reach the beach is along the cliff path from St Peter Port. Allow 1½ hours for the 2-mile (3-km) route.

Start from Guernsey's South Esplanade, and follow the roadside footpath as far as the entrance to the Aquarium *(see page 22)*, following the steps that lead up the cliff face to the left of the museum. Catch your breath by admiring the views from **Clarence Battery**, whose entrance is found near the top of the path. As you will discover, this headland is covered in Napoleonic-era fortifications.

From the Battery, continue uphill (a path off to the left will take you down to tiny **Soldier's Bay**, with its sheltered beach of shingle and sand). To the right and ahead as you climb are some of the walls of **Fort George**, which you will encounter repeatedly on this walk. This massive Georgian fort was built from 1782 to house Guernsey's main garrison and to take over from Castle Cornet *(see page 19)* as the island's main stronghold, overlooking the approaches to St Peter Port. The granite walls now protect an upmarket housing estate, built in the 1960s.

Turn left when you meet the tarmac road called La Corniche to follow the clifftop road for 400 yards, past balconied houses on Guernsey's largest open market estate a cross between the South of France and Los Angeles.

Where La Corniche bends to the right, the cliff path continues left, with fine views back to Soldier's Bay. Further fortifications line the path to the right as you climb away from the cliffs through woodland. At the next path junction, go left to descend through woods that are a haze of blue in spring when the bluebells flower. At the next junction turn left to climb to the clifftop again. As you follow the cliff path you will pass the **Ozanne Steps**, built by a former governor of Guernsey to provide access to a rock platform where swimmers come to take a dip.

Continue along the path until you come to a junction: go straight ahead, up the concrete steps, and turn left to follow a tarmac path which rounds the cliffs to give breathtaking views over **Fermain Bay**, Guernsey's prettiest beach, bobbing with boats and washed by gentle waves. Stretching into the distance, the pine-clad slopes of St Martin's Point add to the impression that this could be the Italian Riviera or the Adriatic coast.

To one side, now serving as a popular beach café, is a Napoleonic-era **tower**. After refreshing yourself here, and perhaps taking a dip, you have a choice for the return journey. If you have walked far enough, you could head up the valley behind the Bay to reach Fort Road and wait for one of the buses that pass at regular intervals. Alternatively, you can walk back via the Fort George Military Cemetery and Belvedere House. To reach the cemetery, retrace your path past the Ozanne Steps. At the next junction, turn left and follow the woodland path that climbs steeply to the terraced **cemetery**. Here in this delightful woodland spot are buried some of the British soldiers who lost their lives in World War I, plus the remains of 111 German soldiers who died here during the Occupation (many of them when Fort George, which served as a Luftwaffe Radar Defence station during World War II, was bombed by the RAF).

From the top terrace, with its war memorial, head along the tarmac road that leads, between high granite walls, back to the Fort George housing estate. Passing manicured lawns and trim hedges, take the first right turn, then left, then straight on until you reach the imposing **gatehouse** to Fort George, with its 1812 date and the name of Sir John Doyle, Lieutenant-Governor of Guernsey *(see page 43)*.

Do not go through the gate, but turn your back on it and go left, past the entrance to Charlotte Battery and on down to the expanse of green known as **Belvedere Field**, once the parade ground for the British garrison. Belvedere House (private) stands graciously over to the right, and a path runs left, down the side of the field, to a **viewpoint** from which there are breathtaking views over St Peter Port and Castle Cornet. Turning your back on the view, go left and look for a path that leads left after 30 yards. This will take you back to the South Esplanade.

Walkers at Fermain Bay

41

Military Cemetery

Castle Cornet close-up

The Pea Stacks off Jerbourg Point

Birdwatchers

Walk 2: Jerbourg Peninsula

The whole of Guernsey's delightfully undeveloped south coast can be explored by means of cliff paths that extend for some 28 miles (45km) from St Peter Port round to the Pleinmont Headland. Following this short stretch may tempt you to tackle the whole route. Allow 2½ hours for the 3½-mile (6-km) route.

Take the road that goes all the way to the tip of the Jerbourg peninsula, where there is a car park, toilets and a kiosk. To the left of the car park, the roof of the German Naval Battery Command Bunker provides a good lookout point for views to St Peter Port, and across to the island of Herm. Cross the car park to the right and follow the tarmac road between the Hotel Jerbourg and the cliff top. Where the road bends right, just beyond a granite memorial to Bill Green, look for a path that leads off to the left.

This descends towards a German bunker – one of several along this route, all sited to take advantage of the panoramic views. The second bunker you pass is now used as a **bird-watching hide**, and maintained by the Royal Society for the Protection of Birds. From here you can (with binoculars) watch nesting gulls and shags on the nearby rock stacks, and linnets and whitethroats feeding among the cliff-top vegetation.

Continue along the path and eventually you will reach a memorial to Sir Victor Gosselin, in whose memory the land around here was donated to the island of Guernsey. Straight ahead there are views of **Moulin Huet Bay**, which you now approach, continuing down the cliff path, while aeroplanes fly in overhead on the approach to Guernsey's airport. Turn left where the cliff path joins a tarmac path, then left again after 20 yards, and left again shortly after. Keep taking the left turn each time a junction appears, passing several German bunkers. Over to the right you will see the obelisk of the Doyle Monument, to which we shall return at the end of the walk.

The cliff path next meets a concrete path – turn left here and follow the path down to a junction. The path to the left goes down to **Petit Port**, which is excellent for bathing when the tide rolls out to reveal firm sand. Our route goes right along the cliff and left at the next junction. The path reaches some steps and comes out onto a tarmac road: go left and downhill to rejoin the cliff path, past a small spring feeding a stream whose waters add lushness to wooded valley. On the left, the granite wall of the **Le Vallon estate** has strategically placed railings, allowing you a view of the ponds and fine gardens beyond the wall.

As you return to the clifftop, you are greeted by a superb view over to the left of the rock formations known as

Les Tas de Pois d'Amont (The Pea Stacks of the East). How they acquired this curious (and far from accurate) name is hard to imagine. The rocks look like monks, with stooped backs and deep pointed hoods – especially the middle stack, which is known as Le Petit Bouan Homme d'Andriou (The Little Good Man Andrew).

The path now passes through holm-oak woodland and eventually emerges at a tarmac road, by a pink and white farmhouse. The path to the left descends to the picturesque **Moulin Huet Bay** *(see page 27)* with its tea garden, and its striking rock formations. The artist Pierre-Auguste Renoir was captivated by the bay's rock pools, cliffs and sea caves: he painted no fewer than 15 pictures of the scenic cove on a painting trip to Guernsey in 1883.

Moulin Huet Bay

No less scenic is the pretty lane to the right, the original site of the Moulin Huet windmill, after which the Bay is named. If you walk up the lane, you can enjoy the sounds of gurgling water from a stream that is channelled along the right-hand side of the road.

Our route back lies up the even prettier **water lane** that leads off from the right-hand side of the car park, with another gurgling stream running in a stone-lined channel to the left. The path climbs steeply and narrows until there is just room to pass between steep, moss-covered banks (Guernsey folk-legend has lanes like this as the abode of fairies, and you can well understand why).

All too soon the path ends at a little granite shelter that protects the spring feeding the water lane. Alongside is a fine group of 17th-century farmhouses, one with a good example of a five-stone Guernsey arch over the front door. Here you should turn right to take the narrow tarmac path signposted Route Fainel, which passes between the farms. The lane emerges at a pretty **parish pump**, dated 1828, and a delightful neo-Gothic house whose wooden front doors are carved with windblown palm trees.

Walking along the peninsula

Turn left by the house to emerge onto a road. Turn right along the road, and left at the next junction. After a short distance you will meet the main Route de Jerbourg road. Turn right here to follow the main road.

A short way beyond the pub, climb the mound up to the **Doyle Monument** for far-reaching coastal views. Named after Sir John Doyle, Lieutenant-Governor of Guernsey from 1803–16, this tower is a post-war replacement of the original, which the Germans demolished to prevent its use as a clandestine signal station. It was under Doyle's supervision that the modern road network on Guernsey was laid down – principally to allow for rapid troop movements at a time of continuing hostilities from France.

The Doyle Monument

From here, the fastest route back to the car park is simply to follow the main road.

Approaching Herm Harbour

New arrivals

Route 5

Herm

Shell Beach – Fisherman's Beach – Herm Common – Belvoir Bay – Herm Manor – St Tugual's chapel – Rosière Steps *See map on page 45*

Herm is a great destination for people who like birds, beaches, walking or food. Food lovers come over to Herm in the summer by the early evening boat to enjoy the almost Mediterranean ambience of the island's waterside restaurants. Here they can indulge in locally farmed oysters and tiny sweet Herm mussels, freshly caught lobster and a variety of fish, as well as Sark lamb and a whole range of organically produced vegetables and daily products. The White House Hotel (tel: 01481 722159) is especially noted for the quality of the food in its Conservatory Restaurant and the more informal Ship Inn next door (no bookings taken for the latter; *see pages 67 and 68*).

Even if you are not a bird lover before you go to Herm you may well undergo a conversion once you reach the island – it is best to take binoculars and a bird identification book, just in case. The island is especially rich in bird life during the spring and autumn migration periods, when the Channel Islands serve as a feeding ground for birds of passage. During spring and summer, the whole island is alive with the vibrant song of larks and wrens, whitethroats and warblers. The cliffs to the south of the island attract nesting puffins and fulmars, while the sand dunes to the north are home to a colony of sand martins and, if you arrive by the early morning boat before the beaches become crowded, you will see whole flocks of oyster catchers, probing the sands for food with their bright orange beaks.

By mid-morning in summer, the beach lovers begin to arrive, heading for the broad swathes of sandy beach to the north and east. Most famous of all is Shell Beach *(see page 45)*, considered by some to be the Channel Islands' best beach, although, in truth, all the beaches on Herm are as good. Shell Beach consists almost entirely of shells, though most have been pulverised to fragments of sand by centuries of wave action. Each tide brings in a new crop of delicate pink, yellow and luminescent shells to keep beachcombers happy. As you explore, however, you will discover that Shell Beach is by no means unique: all the island's beaches have a large amount of shells, as does the island soil – Herm is just one big trap for exotic shells washed here from warmer waters by strong currents and the action of the Gulf Stream. But beware, Herm has the highest level of sunburn in the Channel Islands. Coat yourself, and especially children, liberally with sun cream.

Beach paraphernalia

If you come to Herm unprepared for swimming, you can always buy costumes, snorkels and other beach paraphernalia from the shops near the harbour, and you can hire folding seats from the beach huts on Shell and Belvoir beaches. Not that shopping is a reason for coming to the island: there are no High Street chains here – just a handful of small shops stocked with tasteful seaside souvenirs.

Fisherman's Beach

Freedom from consumer values is what makes Herm so appealing and, with a ban on cars, ghetto-blasters, radios played in public and unseemly behaviour, this really is the place to get away from it all. To make the most of all this peace, the best thing to do is walk around the island. From the harbour, a broad level path leads left, passing the **Mermaid Tavern** (a good spot for lunch, *see page 67*) heading north. The path was once a railway that carried stone from the island's numerous quarries to cargo boats in the harbour. Herm's granite was said to be the hardest and best of all stone quarried in the Channel Islands in the 19th century. It was used for railway construction as well as for more prestigious projects: in London, the Duke of York steps, leading off Pall Mall, and the steps up to St Paul's Cathedral are both made of Herm granite.

To the left, as you follow the path, is ★★ **Fisherman's Beach**, a fine stretch of sand at low tide, when you can also see the weed-covered crates in which Herm's oysters and mussels are grown. The first main landmark on the northwards route is a small cemetery containing two graves and an almost indecipherable inscription; local legend has it that

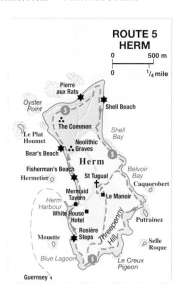

**ROUTE 5
HERM**

0 — 500 m
0 — 1/4 mile

Pierre aux Rats
Oyster Point
Shell Beach
The Common
Le Plat Houmet
Shell Bay
Neolithic Graves
Bear's Beach
Herm
Fisherman's Beach
Hermetier
St Tugual
Belvoir Bay
Caquorobert
Mermaid Tavern
Le Manoir
Herm Harbour
White House Hotel
Threepenny Hill
Putrainez
Mouette
Rosière Steps
Selle Roque
Blue Lagoon
Le Creux Pigeon
Guernsey

The grave of a mother and child

Sea hollies at Shell Beach

this was a mother and child who died of cholera in the early 19th century, buried here by the crew of a passing ship.

Much older tombs lie scattered around ★ **Herm Common**, at the north end of the island, but it is not easy to distinguish them from natural scatters of rock, since these neolithic tombs, dating from the period 3,500 to 2,000BC, have all collapsed – only the regularity of the stones, lying in a rough circle, indicates the site of a former tomb chamber. There were once so many tombs here that archaeologists think Herm was used as a burial isle for members of the Breton nobility. Most were lost to quarrying – to 19th-century quarrymen, the big granite capstones used in the construction of neolithic passage graves were easy picking.

The needle-shaped monument at the northernmost point of the island marks the position of one of the island's more famous dolmens, called the **Pierre aux Rats**. When quarrymen destroyed the massive grave, local seamen were incensed at the loss of such an important landmark and navigational aid, so the obelisk was erected in its place.

★★★ **Shell Beach** lies over to the right, backed by dunes on which prickly sea hollies grow. The common itself is covered in burnet rose, another rare plant that enjoys the Herm environment, as well as all kinds of other wildflowers, from massed primroses in spring, to purple foxglove spires in summer.

If you continue round the coast, you will come to ★★★ **Belvoir Bay** with its refreshment kiosk. This has a smaller but more sheltered beach than those further north. From here you can head south along the undulating (and at times steep) cliff path, which encircles the island and gives access to some of the its best bird-watching points.

Alternatively, you can head up the steep track to the ★ **chapel, manor and farm** at the centre of the island. The battlemented tower at the summit of the hill serves as a landmark as you climb. The tower and manor are the work of Prince Blücher von Wahlstatt, the wealthy German aristocrat, who fell in love with the island in 1890 (neither the first nor the last to do so) and bought the lease. Many of the mature trees on the island were planted by the Prince, who, sadly, was interned at the outbreak of World War I and never returned to Herm. A subsequent tenant was the novelist, Sir Compton Mackenzie, who lived here from 1920, until he retired to the neighbouring island of Jethou, to be succeeded by Lord Perry, Chairman of the Ford Motor Company.

During the war, the island escaped fortification, and was largely left to decay, so that the first post-war tenant spent a small fortune restoring the island farms. Even so, much remained to be done when Peter and Jenny Wood became tenants in 1949; the story of how they fell in love with Herm, and worked to create the thriving island economy of today, based on the twin pillars of tourism and farming, is told in the late Jenny Wood's delightful book, *Herm, Our Island Home*. The island is now managed by John and Julia Singer. They met on Herm 14 years ago and fell in love with the island.

Some of the farm buildings at the top of the hill have been converted to holiday accommodation, but you can visit the little Norman chapel of **St Tugual** in the grounds, with its pretty garden and its memorial to Jenny Wood. Returning uphill and turning right to pass the Manor, you will pass the farm workshops, with dismembered tractors lying around the yard. At the gate to the Manor is a reminder that oxen were once used as draft animals before Lord Perry introduced the first tractors. The ★ **oxen stocks** were used to hold the animals while they were shod, since, unlike horses, bullocks are unable to stand on three legs, and need supporting.

Alongside the Manor you will see another tower, made romantic with fairytale turrets, that was once the island's mill. It, like the chapel, may have been built by the medieval monks who farmed Herm until the Dissolution. They also made the walls of massive granite boulders that line the spine road crossing the centre of the island.

If you follow this, you will pass the island's campsite and eventually rejoin the coastal path at the southern tip of the island. Turn right here, enjoying the views across to Jethou, and you will come to ★ **Rosière Steps**, used by Herm ferries as an alternative landing point when the receding tide makes it impossible to use the main harbour. The path now skirts the gardens of the White House Hotel, backed by the cliffs formed by quarrying activity in the 19th century. Drunken quarrymen were incarcerated in the small beehive-shaped ★ **lock-up** by the tennis courts in the grounds of the **White House Hotel**, which merits inclusion in the *Guinness Book of Records* as Britain's smallest gaol.

Chapel of St Tugual
Oxen stocks

47

Herm cottages

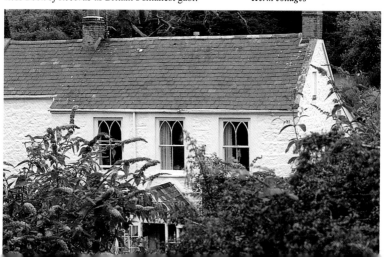

Sark's famous horse-drawn carriages

Route 6

Sark

Horse-drawn carriages – St Peter's Church – Seigneurie Gardens – Port du Moulin – Sark Occupation and Heritage Museum – Dixcart Bay – Grand Grève – Venus Pool *See map on page 50*

Victor Hugo considered Sark to be a *'la plus belle'* (the most beautiful) of the Channel Islands. See if you agree by taking a day trip to the island, or even an overnight stay. Ferries to the island are run by the Isle of Sark Shipping Company and depart several times a day from St Peter Port harbour. The 8am (cheap day return) sailing is popular (and the 4pm coming back) so it's prudent to book for these sailings (tel: 01471 724059) in the height of the season.

The journey to Sark takes 45 minutes and passes south of Herm before swinging northwards past the island of **Brecqhou**, purchased in 1993 as a private tax haven by the wealthy and reclusive Barclay brothers. Their massive Gothic castle, completed in 1998, is clearly visible as the ferry swings to the north of Sark and then comes in close beneath that island's towering cliffs, past rocks from which cormorants and shags launch themselves on fishing flights. As you approach the harbour, you will also see fishermen laying crab and lobster pots, and numerous sea caves and evocatively shaped rocks, as well as the lighthouse on Sark's eastern flank.

What you will not see is any sign of human habitation, for Sark's houses all lie at the centre of the island, in a sheltered hollow, hidden from sight as you approach by sea. To reach the main village, you must climb the steep path from the harbour. The delightful walk passes up the flower and

Boats in the harbour

fern-lined banks of a tree-shaded stream. If you don't want to walk, you can hop on the so-called 'toast rack' – an open-sided tractor-drawn cart, which makes light of the short but steep haul up the hill. Footpath and road merge at the Avel du Creux Hotel, with its Lobster restaurant (tel: 01481 832036). Alongside is the granite engine shed that houses Sark's electricity generator. At the end of the Avenue, next to the tiny two-cell gaol, you will come to the **Sark Visitors' Centre** (high season Mon–Sat 9am–5pm, Sun 9am–1pm, spring and autumn Mon–Sat 10am–4.30pm, winter Mon–Fri 9am–1pm), a source of maps and information on which beaches to try (depending on the state of the tides and the direction of the prevailing wind). Exhibitions on Sark are held here six times a year.

The 'toast rack'

More restaurants (and duty-free shops advertising keener prices than are available on Guernsey) line the short stretch of road that leads up to Sark's main crossroads. It is here that Sark's famous ★★★ **horse-drawn carriages** (the only kind of transport allowed on the island, apart from tractors and bicycles) wait for passengers. Place yourself in the hands of a driver and you will be looked after for the next 2½ hours or so, as a knowledgeable guide takes you to the island's main sights (you can pre-book an island tour when you book your ferry crossing, or you can book when you arrive). Alternatively, you can head up Sark's main street, called the Avenue, and hire a bicycle at the hire shop on the right – or you can simply trust to your own two feet.

49

The Avenue divides the island into two halves – to the north the highlights are the Seigneurie gardens, the lighthouse and the Occupation Museum; to the south, wooded lanes lead to La Coupée, the vertiginous landbridge linking what some describe as the separate islands of Little and Great Sark.

Northern Sark

Head up the Avenue, with its souvenir shops and general stores (and stock up with picnic ingredients here if you do not plan to eat in one of the island's several pubs and farmhouse cafés). At the top of the Avenue, by the Post Office, turn right, and continue right at the next junction. You will shortly come to ★★ **St Peter's Church**, built in 1820. The simple building has stained-glass windows of various saints, including St Magloire, who came from Dol in Brittany in 565 to found a monastery on Sark. The monastery flourished, supporting 62 monks and serving as a school for the children of the Breton nobility, until marauding Viking pirates destroyed the buildings and killed the monks in the 9th century.

Stained glass in St Peter's Island Hall

Turning right out of the church, you will pass the **Island Hall**, which serves as a sports club for the island's children and as a centre for the island's social life. Alongside is the stone building that houses Sark's parliament,

known as the Chief Pleas. Sark's constitution dates back to 1563, when Heleret de Carteret was granted sovereignty over the island in return for maintaining a militia, whose chief task was to keep the island free of the pirates who had been using Sark as a base from which to harass English shipping. Heleret took 40 Jerseymen with him to colonise the uninhabited island. The feudal form of government set up in Elizabeth I's reign prevailed right up until 2008 when the island held its first general election and a new democratic Chief Pleas was sworn in.

The present Seigneur lives in the Seigneurie, which lies a little further to the north, along a broad straight line which passes the farm called La Moinerie where Magloire's

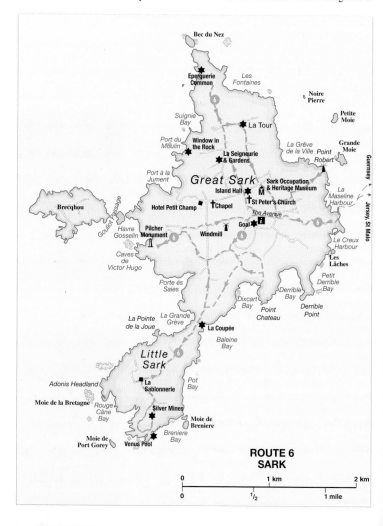

ROUTE 6
SARK

monastery once stood. You will share this road with numerous horses and carriages, all heading to or from the ★★★ **Seigneurie Gardens** (Apr–Oct daily 10am–5pm). The walled gardens surrounding the Seigneurial home are packed with colourful flowers and shrubs, including climbing roses and exotic plants, such as gazanias, canna lilies and bottle-brush plants from New Zealand, that flourish in the frost-free island environment. The house itself (not open to the public) is no less exotic, with the Dutch gables of its Victorian wing added to the original house of 1732 and a large watchtower, built (so it is said) for sending signals to Guernsey in 1854.

Seigneurie Gardens

To the rear of the house is the Battery, where a cider apple crusher and several historic cannons are displayed alongside an ornate tower, and a turreted 18th-century dovecote (one of the Seigneur's sole privileges was to keep pigeons and doves, which fed freely and with impunity on the crops of the tenants). There is also a small area of woodland to explore, with a series of duck-filled ponds.

A short way along the track north of the Seigneurie is a left turn that leads down, through woods, to ★ **Port du Moulin** (once the site of the watermill), with its fine coastal scenery. Just before you get to the beach, look out for the artificial 'Window in the Rock', a square hole cut through the cliff to allow carts to descend to the beach and gather *vraic*, or seaweed, used for fertilising the Seigneur's fields and garden. Returning to the main track, you can turn left and continue to the end of the road to ★ **L'Eperquerie Common**, at the northern tip of the island, named after the poles *(perques)* once erected here for drying fish.

Window in the Rock

Coming back, turn left down Rue de Fort, to the Napoleonic-era defensive works at **La Tour**, then turn right (south) heading back to the centre of Sark. Take the second left turn, which leads past the Mermaid Tavern down to Point Robert and Sark's ★★ **lighthouse**. It was built in 1912 and stands halfway down the cliff into which it nestles, down a flight of 165 steps but still 213ft (65m) above high water mark. It is now fully automatic and from the platform, offers superb views of Maseline Harbour and on a clear day, France.

Returning back to the main street, turn right into Rue Lucas to visit the ★**Sark Occupation and Heritage Museum** (Apr–Oct, erratic opening hours, but theoretically Mon–Sat 11am–1pm, 2–4pm). The displays include old farming implements and photographs of island life, along with numerous relics of the Occupation. Sark suffered less than the other Channel Islands during the war, partly because the indomitable Seigneur, Dame Sybil Hathaway, deployed her fluent German and forceful personality to ensure that island life continued along as normal a course as possible during this difficult period.

The gaol

Southern Sark

One of the pictures in the museum shows German prisoners of war reinforcing the track across La Coupée in 1945. This narrow isthmus, with sheer drops either side, is Sark's most famous site, linking the two parts of the island.

To reach it, head down the Avenue and turn left at the end. You will pass, on the left, a curious stone building with the prominent date of 1856: this is the two-cell island ★ **gaol**, built to hold miscreants at a time when Sark's quarrying industry (and the incidence of drunkenness and violence) were at a peak. Turn left at the next junction and you will pass, on the right, one of the oldest buildings on the island. Now divided into several cottages, this ★ **longhouse** was the home of Heleret de Carteret after he colonised the island in 1563 (round the corner is the fine house his descendants built in the 17th century, with the de Carteret coat of arms in the western gable).

At the next path, turn left, following signs to the Stocks and Dixcart Hotels. At the valley bottom, keep right on the path to the Stocks Hotel, then right up to the main road, before turning left into the grounds of the Dixcart (pronounced *Deecart*) Hotel. Passing the Dixcart Hotel, head up the lane to the sharp right bend.

Here you can make a detour to ★★ **Dixcart Bay** by taking the path to the left of the green field gate and heading down the steep woodland path to the valley bottom; follow the stream from here until it reaches the bay – a fine spot for bathing when the tide is out. To return, head back up the stream, then take the path to the left which climbs steeply to the clifftop above the bay and curves round to meet the road again at a pair of green gates.

If you are not taking the detour, turn right for the same pair of green gates, which are at the next angle in the road. Cross the stile between the two gates and follow the field-

La Coupée

edge path to the next stile. The path now enters a tunnel of blackthorn and bracken. As you emerge, the path bears right and ★★★ **La Coupée** soon comes into sight, looking just like a miniature stretch of the Great Wall of China.

A roadway tops this knife-edge ridge, some 10ft (3m) wide – just sufficient for a horse and carriage to cross. To either side there is a nearly sheer drop of 260ft (80m) straight to the sea. Crossing La Coupée was once extremely hazardous but, as the plaque in the middle of the causeway relates, the path was made good with concrete and handrails in 1945 by German prisoners of war. A steep flight of steps leads down from La Coupée to ★★ **Grand Grève** beach on the right, where you can bathe when the tide is out.

Grand Grève beach

Alternatively, you can continue south to explore Little Sark, enjoying views of the neighbouring islands as you follow the sunken lane across the top to La Sablonnerie, a fine hotel with a restaurant and charming tea gardens, and the ivy-covered ruins of a windmill nearby. Turn left by the hotel and continue along the track until the tall chimneys of Sark's now abandoned ★ **silver mines** come into view. The mines produced both silver and copper, but not in sufficient quantities to be an economic success and, in 1847, soon after the galleries collapsed and flooded, the ill-fated mining company went bankrupt.

53

Go through the gate and head towards the first of the chimneys, then follow the path as it bends left. The objective is to reach ★ **Venus Pool**, a large natural rock pool at the base of the nearby cliffs. When the grass runs out and gives way to bare granite, cairns mark the best route. Reaching the pool involves a scramble, but you can pay homage to the goddess of love by bathing in the pool, or you can enjoy the many other smaller tide pools, with their crystal-clear waters and coral-like weeds.

To return to La Coupée there is only one way – the way you came. Back on Great Sark, carry straight on along the main track, until you reach a crossroads after about half a mile (1km). The first left turn leads to the **Pilcher Monument** (built to commemorate Joseph Pilcher, who drowned while crossing to Guernsey in a storm in 1868). From here there are fine views back to Guernsey. The right turn opposite leads down Rue de Moulin, named after the ★ **windmill**, built by Helier de Carteret in 1571. In use until 1919, it stands at the highest point on the island, at 365ft (111m), and just a short step away from the island's main street.

*The Pilcher Monument
Cottage gardens*

If you have time when returning to the harbour, turn right and go through the rock-cut tunnel, dug in 1588, to view Sark's original dock, pretty Creux Harbour, which was replaced by the modern port, La Maseline, in 1947.

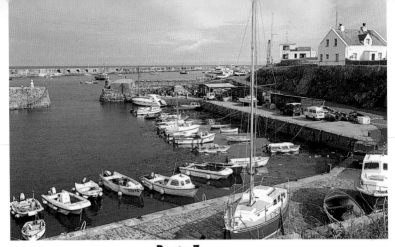

Braye harbour

Route 7

Alderney

The quick way to Alderney: Aurigny Air Services

Braye – St Anne – Alderney Museum – Island Hall – Fort Albert – Hammond Memorial – Corblets Bay – Mannez Lighthouse – Longis Bay – L'Etacs – Telegraph Bay *See map on page 55*

Alderney is the third largest of the Channel Islands – large enough for day trippers to leave feeling that they could have done with a little more time, yet easily small enough to feel like an island, with the sea nearly always in view. If you come on a day trip from any of the other islands, or indeed from France, you will have approximately four hours to fill. Taxis and buses will be waiting at the harbour offering inexpensive round-the-island tours (call Island Taxis, tel: 01481 823823).

Hiring a car is not really necessary, but you might consider hiring a bicycle at Puffin Cycles (tel: 01481 823725) on Braye Street, right by the harbour, or at several other outlets in the town of St Anne. Another alternative is to hire a two-seater golf-style buggy, which will carry you up and down the island's hills at a sedate 10 miles (16km) per hour (you need a full driving licence to hire one, and to be over 21 years of age; tel: 01481 822606).

Braye and the breakwater

There are several attractions in the immediate vicinity of the harbour, in the one-street village of ★ **Braye**. First there is the great sandy sweep of Braye Bay, right next to the harbour, which is protected by the Alderney breakwater and therefore offers safe and sheltered bathing. Braye itself offers a number of places to eat, from chip shops and pubs to up-market seafood restaurants, and there are supermarkets and off-licences selling duty-free goods. To the right of the harbour, Channel Jumper sells island knitwear.

The ★ **breakwater**, along with Alderney's ring of 12 defensive fortifications, is a legacy of the hostility and suspicion that existed between England and France in the early 19th century, even though hostilities officially ceased after the defeat of Napoleon. When the French began constructing a naval harbour at Cherbourg, alarm bells rang in the Admiralty, and the British government suddenly discovered the urgent necessity of building 'harbours of refuge' at Braye in Alderney, as well as on Guernsey and Jersey. The intention was to convert Braye harbour into a massive naval base, with two breakwaters at each side of the bay. Only the western wall was built, completed in 1847 and originally a mile long. Battered by massive waves (signs on the entrance to the breakwater warn walkers that the wall is liable to sudden swamping by breaking waves), part of the breakwater was abandoned and now lies submerged, a hazard to shipping, beneath the waves. The 1,000-yd stretch that survives requires constant maintenance, using stone brought here by rail from Mannez Quarry at the northern tip of the island.

The breakwater

At weekends and on bank holidays from Easter to September, when the ★★ **railway** is not in use for carrying granite, it carries passengers on a 2-mile (3-km) trip from the harbour to the quarry, a journey of 15 minutes' duration (these depart at 2pm, 3pm and 4pm; for information tel: 01481 823580 or visit www.alderneyrailway.com). Passengers are either carried in a diesel-powered railcar, or one of two 1938 London Underground carriages. The bright

Carriages from the Underground

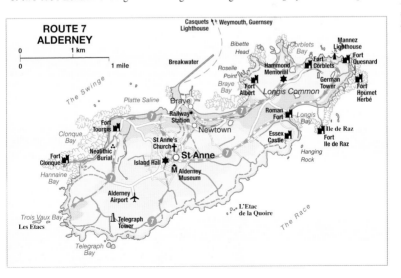

ROUTE 7
ALDERNEY

0   1 km
0   1 mile

Casquets ⚓ Weymouth, Guernsey
Lighthouse

Bibette Head
Corblets Bay
Mannez Lighthouse
Fort Quesnard
Breakwater
Roselle Point
Hammond Memorial
Fort Corblets
German Tower
Fort Houmet Herbé
The Swinge
Platte Saline
Braye Bay
Fort Albert
Longis Common
Braye
Railway Station
Roman Fort
Longis Bay
Fort Tourgis
Clonque Bay
Newtown
Essex Castle
Ile de Raz
Fort Ile de Raz
Neolithic Burial
St Anne's Church
St Anne
Hanging Rock
Fort Clonque
Island Hall
Alderney Museum
Hannaine Bay
Alderney Airport
Trois Vaux Bay
Les Etacs
Telegraph Tower
L'Etac de la Quoire
The Race
Telegraph Bay

St Anne

Old Church tower and Museum

red tube trains shuttling beneath the gorse and bracken covered hills of Longis Common make a bizarre sight.

St Anne – the island capital

From Braye harbour, it is a short uphill stroll to the main town, St Anne (locals simply refer to it as 'The Town'). ★★★ **St Anne** consists of a maze of cobbled streets, lined by houses of granite and sandstone, many of them whitewashed or painted in pastel shades of pink, cream, yellow and blue. Victoria Street (given this name when the monarch visited Alderney on 9 August 1854) has the tourist information office and most of Alderney's shops and restaurants. Climbing up the hill, you will pass the entrance to ★★ **St Anne's Church** on the right – this massive French-style building of local granite, with Caen stone details, was designed by Sir George Gilbert Scott in 'chaste Gothic' style, and opened in 1850. It replaced the tiny old church, which was described at the time as 'small and mean'.

The body of the ★ **Old Church** was demolished, but you will find the squat tower, which survived, and the old churchyard, containing some fine 18th-century tombstones, by continuing to the top of Victoria Street and then turning right into the High Street. The tower and churchyard stand next door to the ★★★ **Alderney Museum** (Apr–Oct Mon–Fri 10am–noon and 2.30–4.30pm, Sat–Sun 10am–noon), which is housed in the former Ecole Publique, founded in 1790 by the island's governor, Jean Le Mesurier. The museum provides a detailed account of the island, from its geology and wildlife to such fascinating topics as whether the Alderney cow ever existed as a distinctive breed.

One section of the museum deals with wartime Alderney and the evacuation of all but a handful of the island's population. When the islanders were allowed to return in the winter of 1945, they had to agree to work cooperatively, under central management, to restore houses and farmland left derelict by the occupying forces. Hard work and self-sacrifice saw the island economy restored within two years, but there were moments of farce, as illustrated by the infamous Battle of Braye. This took place in 1945 after British troops, preparing for the islanders' return, cleaned out their homes and stacked such furniture as had survived in the open air, with a rope barrier. A free-for-all broke loose once the rope was removed, with islanders' fighting each other for their possessions. For decades after, it is said, some people on the island refused to invite others into their homes for fear that their guest might recognise a family heirloom.

Another part of the museum displays artefacts salvaged from the Elizabethan warship, the *Makeshift*, which marine archaeologists are excavating off the north coast of the island. Apart from a cannon, pottery and leather clothing, two of the most intriguing finds are early tobacco pipes

– one made of pottery and one of pewter – with tiny bowls, reflecting the fact that tobacco, introduced to Europe only two decades previously, was still a very expensive luxury.

Close to the museum are some of Alderney's oldest and most dignified buildings: turning right just beyond the museum will take you into Connaught Square, with the Old Government House of 1763, now better known as ★ **Island Hall**, the place where the States of Alderney, the island parliament, holds its meetings. The imposing Georgian building was originally built as a private house for the Le Mesuriers, hereditary governors of Alderney, who had clawed their way to wealth and status through acts of licensed piracy. In one year alone during the wars with France, John Le Mesurier, under a licence granted by the English Crown, captured shipping valued at £135,000 (a fortune in the late 18th century).

Island Hall

The island's northeastern coast

With energy and determination, you could just tour the whole of Alderney in a day. If you have longer to spend, it is better to split the island into two. The road system on Alderney encourages this, with a circular road that hugs the northeastern coast, forming a loop from Braye back to St Anne. Following the Lower Road east out of Braye, you will skirt Braye Bay and encounter ★ **Fort Albert**, the first in the chain of 12 fortresses encircling the island. These were designed by Captain William Jervois in the 1840s and 50s as part of the same defensive works as the Alderney breakwater. Because the English were suspicious of French intentions, they imported hundreds of English and Irish labourers to the island to construct these fine fortifications of pink granite, most of which were never subsequently garrisoned. Several have now been converted into private flats and holiday apartments, so there is no public access, while others remain in a decayed and dangerous state – best appreciated from afar. Fort Albert is perhaps the finest of all the forts, and it is well positioned to defend Braye Harbour.

57

Braye Bay and Fort Albert

A short way on, the road divides and the spot is marked by the ★ **Hammond Memorial**, commemorating the many prisoners of war who died on Alderney during the Occupation period. They were imported to work as slave labourers on the construction of the defences that were to turn the Channel Islands into the most heavily fortified area in Europe. Plaques in Hebrew, Polish, Russian and Spanish indicate the origins of the those who lost their lives: Spanish partisans who were on the losing side in the Civil War, Jews from Alsace and Czechoslovakia, and prisoners of war from Russia and Poland.

Hammond Memorial plaques

Visible as you continue northwards is a large and sinister fire control tower, built by the Germans to act as a command post for the artillery batteries around the island.

Mannez Quarry and Lighthouse

Longis Bay

From this spot there are clear views across the Race of Alderney to Cap de la Hague, in Normandy.

Evidence of quarrying activity lies all around this north-eastern tip of the island, with fresh stone lying in heaps at ★ **Mannez Quarry**, near to the railway station terminus. The geology can be studied in closer detail in the exposed rocks of delightful ★★ **Corblets Bay**, with its clean sands and shallow waters. Alongside the bay is the ★★ **Mannez Lighthouse**, which is open to the public at weekends from late May to late September, offering fine views from the lantern.

Continuing round the coast, another fine stretch of sandy beach is found at ★★ **Longis Bay**. Here additional shelter is provided by the massive concrete anti-tank wall. This was constructed by the Germans who were convinced that the Allies would eventually try to retake the Channel Islands by landing tanks and troops on this coast. At the far end of Longis Bay, an attractive château-like building, known locally as the Nunnery, stands on the site of Alderney's Roman fort. It was from here that the coins, pottery and bronze work in Alderney Museum were excavated, while much of the museum's Iron-Age material came from a nearby site on the adjacent golf course.

The Nunnery marks the point at which Alderney's lowlands give out. Just to the south, the cliffs rise steeply to the prominent landmark known as the **Hanging Rocks**. Here, two huge boulders look as if they have detached themselves from the cliff and are about to tumble into the sea. One local story has it that Jerseymen, jealous of Alderney's beauty, once tried to tow the island closer to their own by attaching a rope to the rocks; all they succeeded in doing was to tilt the rocks. **Essex Castle**, now a private home, stands high above the rocks, while the main road leads straight uphill, back to St Anne.

The south of the island

Alderney's open and unenclosed landscape has few walls, trees or hedges, preserving as it does the island's medieval open-field system of farming. Farms were clustered together in St Anne, and farmland, which mostly lay to the south and west of the town, was divided into strips, called *riages*. Today, very little of the land is under plough: most is used for grazing by horses, sheep and cows.

The southern part of the island can only properly be explored on foot or by bike, since the best parts of the coast are only accessible along rough paths. Allow two to three hours for exploration, starting in St Anne at the church; take the western exit from the churchyard and turn right to follow the road called La Vallée down to the sea at Saline Bay. Turn left to follow the coast road past **Fort Tourgis**, where there are signs warning visitors to keep out of this massive and unrestored fortress.

Take the road to the right of the fort to follow the coast around its base. The surfaced road soon gives way to a track, leading to **Fort Clonque**, built in 1854 and picturesquely sited on an offshore islet. The fort has been converted to holiday accommodation by the Landmark Trust *(see page 79)*.

Fort Clonque

59

Follow the track from here as it winds uphill giving fine views. Turn left at the next junction, then right onto a surfaced track, which turns back into a rough track after a short distance. Continue along to the end of the headland for a view of the offshore islands called ★★ **L'Etacs**. What looks like snow covering these rocky islets is, in fact, a colony of gannets, which first arrived on the rocks in 1940. They now form a large breeding colony that nests here in spring, departing again every autumn.

Grazing country

Retrace your steps and take the next turn right. Ignore the next right turn, but take the right turn after that to explore ★ **Telegraph Bay**, which is reached by a steep cliff path. If the tide is out, this is a good spot for swimming and sunbathing. The Bay is named after the Telegraph Tower that stands on top of the headland, used in the early 19th century to send semaphore signals to the other islands.

Return to the main track and turn right, skirting the southern side of the airport. The track bends northwards at the far side of the airfield, taking you, via La Petite Rue, back to St Anne's High Street.

Island Voyages

Two and a half-hour tours around the island or weekly day trips with *MV Voyager* (tel: 01481 823666 or 07781 102962) or *MV Lady Mavis II* (tel: 07781 101971), include close-up views of the puffin colonies on the nearby island of **Burhou**, and of the gannets, shags, guillemots, kittiwakes and razorbills that inhabit the inaccessible coves and islets around Alderney's shores.

Island Heritage

Some of the oldest human structures in Europe are to be found on the island of Guernsey. The oldest of all is the passage grave at Les Fouillages, hidden among the bracken on L'Ancresse Common *(see page 38)*. Discovered in 1976, it has been dated to 4,500 BC – making it 1,500 years older than the earliest remains at Stonehenge. Les Fouillages dates from the neolithic era, when Europe's first farmers were beginning to domesticate animals and crops. Before that, Guernsey's hunter-gatherer population probably lived in caves, surviving by the tactic of herding mammoth and woolly rhino together and driving them to their death over cliffs, eating the flesh and using the skins to clothe themselves. Guernsey's neolithic population must have prospered, because the island has many fine tombs dating from the period 3,500 to 2,850 BC. It is not just the number of tombs that is indicative of wealth – they are also constructed from massive blocks of granite, suggesting that the builders must have been able to command considerable resources and control the large numbers of people needed to quarry, transport and lift the stones. The best and most complete on Guernsey is Le Déhus Dolmen *(see page 39)*, with its massive capstone carved with the mysterious figure of a bearded archer, but there are scores of other examples dotted around the coast. For the next 3,000 years on Guernsey, traders and invaders came and went, but none left a permanent mark on the island. Early forts, towns and churches there must have been, but these all now lie buried beneath their modern-day successors.

Norman or English?

Guernsey's historical link with the English Crown began when the unpopular King John lost Normandy to King Philip Augustus of France. With John's defeat, at Rouen on 24 June 1204, the Lordship of the Channel Islands technically passed to France. In reality they were dangerously exposed and with the choice allegiance to the French King or the English Crown. Guernsey's constitutional, administrative and cultural evolution had begun and the islands' unique identity had been born The Channel Islands had become a strategic prize in the cross channel power struggle. Eustace 'the Monk' successfully attacked with some 30 ships, reclaiming them for England in September 1205. Guernsey's fortification began, with the building of Castle Cornet at the entrance to St Peter Port harbour. 'As a result you are rarely out of sight of a fortification of one sort or another, a castle, tower or gun emplacement.'

However, the French soon recaptured the islands, followed by a well-planned English recovery in July 1206. King John courted the islands' loyalty when granted the rights and

Opposite: the Little Chapel, Guernsey

Les Fouillages burial chamber, Guernsey

The Normans in action

Traditional costume

L'Ancresse Bay and tower

privileges they had enjoyed under previous Dukes of Normandy and, just to make sure, took hostages from some of the leading local families. In return he continued to govern in his capacity as Duke of Normandy. Although Henry III abandoned the title of Duke of Normandy, the Treaty of Paris of 1259 confirmed his possession of the Islands. This remains the position today, and Guernsey has never been incorporated into the United Kingdom. But the French continued to attack the Channel Islands and harass the islands' shipping. The last serious attempt to invade was when they were defeated in 10 minutes at the Battle of Jersey in 1781.

Fortress Guernsey

This was to prove the last battle ever to be fought on British soil, but it did not stop the British from remaining suspicious of French intentions, and many of the island's surviving fortifications date from this period: Guernsey's response to the attempted invasion of Jersey was to build a chain of 15 windmill-like coastal towers, all of which survive, to serve as gun emplacements, protecting the beaches where French troops might be expected to land.

Anti-French measures did not stop at coastal defences: the face of Guernsey and its neighbours was reshaped as barracks were built, and troops moved into the islands in their thousands. They were to be joined by the thousands of quarrymen and navvies imported from Britain and Ireland to work on the construction of defences, such as Alderney's huge breakwater, and later on the exploitation of the islands' quarries to provide stone for railway and road construction on the mainland. The quiet islands were transformed, as winding and unpaved rural green lanes were replaced by the straight military roads that serve as the main roads on Guernsey today.

Off the beaten track

Green lanes and fairies

Some of the old green lanes survive, however, and these form a delightful network of paths and bridleways, prohibited to vehicular traffic, linking farms and communities. More delightful still are the few remaining water lanes, where a rushing stream tumbles downhill beside the path, following the course of a granite-lined channel.

Local people regard such lanes as the abode of fairies. By fairies, they do not mean the butterfly-like creatures that inhabit the pages of Arthur Rackham fairy tales, but Shakespeare's fairies – creatures that delight in wreaking havoc in human lives, turning the milk sour, preventing the cream from turning to butter, tripping the horse as it plods down the lane. Greeting the fairies when you enter their realm is one way of ensuring that they will leave you alone – treating them with disrespect, or failing to acknowledge their existence, can lead to disaster.

Festivals

Precise dates of festivals and events vary from year to year, but the tourist offices publish a comprehensive monthly list. The islands promote important culinary events from May to November and Guernsey hosts three floral festival weeks in spring, summer and autumn.

April/May: Wild Flower Fortnight (late Apr–early May) on Sark, with an exhibition and guided walks.

May: Alderney's Milk o' Punch Sunday takes place on the first Sunday in the month. Milk o' Punch is a drink made from milk and egg, with a healthy tot of rum and some mystery ingredients. It is offered free by every pub on the island between noon and 2pm. Each pub has its own recipe, and the objective is to stroll from pub to pub, comparing the brews. Alderney's 10-day Seafood Festival is the island's gastronomic highlight of the year. Guernsey's Walking Week offers a structured programme of walks revealing many aspects of the island's history and character. Liberation Day, on 9 May, commemorates the end of the German Occupation with street entertainment in St Peter Port and a fireworks display over Castle Cornet.

June: Floral Guernsey Festival Week and Show, which includes guided tours of major private gardens, and Sark's Midsummer Show both celebrate the islands' flowers and garden produce with displays and entertainment.

Vaier Marchi at Saumarez Park

July: Held in the grounds of Saumarez Park, Le Vaier Marchi (Old Market) is an opportunity to shop for crafts and food sold by costumed stallholders, and enjoy displays of traditional music and dance. The month-long Seafood Festival offers tastings, demonstrations and the chance to dine out on gourmet seafood. The early part of the month sees Guernsey's second Floral Festival.

August: Alderney Week includes raft races, attempts to fly without the aid of machines, and summer sports, culminating in a torchlit parade and firework display. Guernsey has two agricultural shows: the rural West Show and the North Show, held in Saumarez Park, which includes Guernsey's Battle of Flowers parade, when lavishly decorated floats form a colourful climax to the weekend.

Firefighting in the Battle of Flowers

September: Sark hosts the Grand Autumn show, when local gardening and cooking enthusiasts showcase their produce. Guernsey holds its autumn Floral Festival week. During Battle of Britain week Guernsey mounts a popular air display over St Peter Port harbour.

October: Guernsey's three-day Jazz Festival is held at the end of the month at the Duke of Richmond Hotel.

October/November: During Guernsey's Tennerfest, most hotels and restaurants offer menus at £10, £15 and £20 per diner. Great value seafood if you are there off-season.

Food and Drink

Opposite: lobster pots

Some seriously prosperous people live on Guernsey, with the result that the island has more than its fair share of up-market restaurants, catering as much to well-heeled local people as to visitors. Have no fear, however: at the other end of the scale, there are plenty of more humble establishments, from fish and chip cafés serving the freshest of food to rural pubs offering a range of bar meals.

Freshness guaranteed

Regional cuisine

At its best, Channel Islands food draws on locally produced ingredients and is unbeatable. Oysters, scallops, spider crabs, lobsters and mussels are all caught or farmed locally. Herm mussels make a cheap lunchtime snack and are served in many a pub: though quite small, they are wonderfully tender and sweet. For a full blow out, order a Breton-style *plateau de fruits de mer*, and work your way through a king-size seafood banquet.

Crab cocktail

65

Market gardening thrives on the islands, but even Guernsey dwellers will bend the knee to the deliciously earthy new potatoes grown by rival Jersey and likely to be found on the menu from March onwards. Tomatoes, celery, courgettes, peppers and most other salad ingredients will be locally grown, as will the strawberries, accompanied, as likely as not, by delicious Guernsey cream.

This is likely to find its way into all sorts of dishes, from tea-time scones and cream to soups and sauces, along with the bright-yellow Guernsey butter that will be served with your breakfast toast or spread on a slice of traditional Guernsey *gâche* (fruit loaf, pronounced 'gosh'). Island milk does not, however, make good cheese. Fortunately, with France a short hop away, this is compensated for by a good selection of farmhouse cheeses from Normandy. Fresh French baguettes, the perfect accompaniment to cheese, can be bought from bakers in St Peter Port (try, for example, Boulangerie Victor Hugo in Le Pollet), and some wine merchants sell imported bottles of *cidre bouché*, sparkling farmhouse cider, from Normandy and Brittany – perfect for a beach picnic. For those who prefer locally brewed beer, Randalls have just opened a state-of-the-art brewery at St George's Esplanade, St Peter Port, to brew Breda lager, Patois Cask conditioned ale and Monty's bitter. Tours take place on Saturdays at 9.45am and 11am from April to September and the entrance fee includes a pint of lager or ale (for bookings tel: 01481 720134).

Trailing strawberries

Restaurants

The suggestions starting over the page are listed according to the following categories: **£££** (over £70 for two without drinks); **££** (£45–70); **£** (under £45).

Guernsey

The Auberge, Jerbourg, St Martins, tel: 01481 238485. Consistently excellent food in a modern minimalistic restaurant/bar with stunning views of the surrounding islands. Widely regarded as the 'trendiest' restaurant on the island. **£££**

Auberge du Val, Sous L'Eglise, St Saviours tel: 01481 263862. Very popular traditional auberge in an attractive rural setting. Ideal for a simple bistro-style lunch or more adventurous evening meals. **££**

Café L'Escalier, Le Gouffre, Forest, tel: 01481 264121. Lovely clifftop café/restaurant serving breakfast, lunch, cream teas and casual evening meals. Perfect spot for clifftop walkers in need of respite. **£–££**

The Beach Café at Fermain Bay

Café du Moulin, Rue de Quanteraine, St Pierre du Bois tel: 01481 265944. Cosy rustic restaurant in a peaceful unspoilt valley setting. Lovely outdoor dining terrace. Serves imaginative gastro food. **££–£££**

Christie's, The Pollet, St Peter Port, tel: 01481 726624. Smart continental-style bistro serving anything from a simple café au lait to a set-price lunch or full evening meal. **£**

Christophe, Fort Road, St Peter Port, tel: 01481 230725. Owned by Christophe Vincent, Guernsey's only Michelin starred chef. Conveniently located on the outskirts of St Peter Port. Superb French cuisine in luxurious sophisticated surroundings. **£££**

Da Nello's, 46 The Pollett, St Peter Port, tel: 01481 721552 There are numerous Italian restaurants in Guernsey but Nello's is the favourite with local people. Bustling trattoria serving a wide range of traditional pasta, seafood and meat dishes. **££**

L'Escalier, Tower Hill, St Peter Port, tel: 01481 710088. Small intimate restaurant offering top quality french cuisine. Excellent value five-course Sunday lunch. **£££**

Fermain Beach Café, Fermain Bay, St Peter Port, tel: 01481 238636. A former beach kiosk, now a hugely popular bistro café specialising in seafood. An ideal alfresco lunch venue, overlooking one of Guernsey's prettiest bays. Book two weeks in advance in summer. **££**

Local specialities

Fleur du Jardin, Kings Mills, Castel, tel: 01481 257996. The nearest thing in Guernsey to a genuine 'olde worlde' country pub. Regularly voted Channel Islands dining pub of the year in the *UK Good Pub Guide*. Popular Sunday lunch. **£**

La Frégate, Les Cotils, St Peter Port, tel: 01481 724624 Outstanding slightly formal restaurant with magical views of the harbour and outer islands. International cuisine using local products wherever possible. **£££**

Longfrie Inn, Rue de Longfrie, St Pierre du Bois, tel: 01481 263107. Welcoming family-friendly country pub serving large helpings of traditional pub food. Beer garden and Indoor Fun Factory for the children. **£**

The Ship Inn on Herm

Mora, The Quay, St Peter Port, tel: 01481 715053. Recently opened in former wine cellars, Mora comprises an upstairs restaurant and grill, specialising in Anglo-Norman cuisine, and the downstairs brasserie for coffee, cakes and casual lunches. **££**

Le Nautique, Quay Steps, St Peter Port, tel: 01481 721714 Considered by many to be the island's best, albeit slightly old fashioned, fish restaurant. Emphasis on local seafood – lobster, brill, oysters, etc. **££**

The Pavilion, Le Gron, St Saviours, tel: 01481 264165. Brasserie and tearooms in attractive gardens at the Bruce Russell Silver & Goldsmith Centre. Reasonably priced menu with fantastic puddings and cakes. **£**

Le Petit Bistro, 56 Lower Pollet, St Peter Port, tel: 01481 725055. Authentic French cuisine in Parisian-style bistro. Specialities feature *coq au vin*, Coquille St Jacques and frogs' legs. **££**

Saltwater, Albert Pier, St Peter Port, tel: 01481 720823. Reasonably priced seafood restaurant. Attentive service, good atmosphere and chic decor. Great views over the working harbour and Castle Cornet. Window tables are best but must be booked in advance. **££**

The Swan, St Julian's Avenue, St Peter Port. Newly renovated inn with traditional cosy atmosphere and honest British cuisine. **£–££**

Herm

The Mermaid, Herm Harbour, tel: 01481 710170. The social hub of the island, with pub lunches, pizza in high season and evening meals at the Black Rock Grill where steak and fish are cooked on volcanic rocks at your table. **£–££**

The Ship Inn, Herm Harbour, tel: 01481 722159. Next door to (and part of) the White House, this pub restaurant serves snacks and more elaborate meals. **£**

67

For seafood on Alderney

A Sark favourite

The White House, Herm Harbour, tel: 01481 722159. Try to get a window seat in this conservatory restaurant to enjoy the westward views of the sun setting across the water behind St Peter Port. **££**

Sark

Aval du Creux, tel: 01481 832036. Located at the top of Harbour Hill, the Aval de Creux is well known for its seafood dishes. **££**

Hotel Petit Champ, tel: 01481 832046. located on Sark's west coast the hotel is renowned for its fresh crab and lobster dishes. Lunchtime food ranges from sandwiches and snacks to main meals served in the restaurant or alfresco in the garden. **££**

La Sablonnerie, tel: 01481 832061. Located in the sourthern part of Sark and the perfect place to stop on a walking tour of the island. You can enjoy snacks, cream teas and seafood platters in the flower-filled tea gardens, or a gourmet luncheon in the restaurant, based on the ingredients produced on the hotel's own organic farm. **££**

Stocks Hotel, tel: 01481 832001. Next door to the Dixcart Hotel, Stocks has a pub menu in the Smugglers' Bar and more sophisticated fare in the main restaurant. **£–££**

Alderney

First and Last, Braye Harbour, tel: 01481 823162. This harbourside restaurant, with sea views, boasts the best bouillabaisse in the Channel Islands, plus fresh-caught local oysters, mussels, prawns, lobster, scallops and crab. **££**

Georgian House, Victoria Street, St Anne, tel: 01481 822471. The best place to eat here is in the lovely sheltered garden at the rear of the hotel. The fresh fish tastes all the better for being charcoal grilled. A range of interesting daily specials. **££**

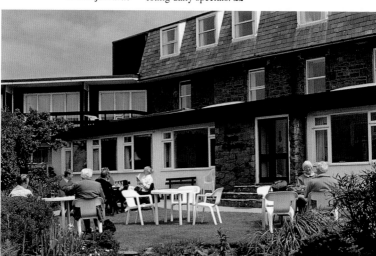

Active Pursuits

Angling

The variety of fish in Guernsey waters numbers nearly 80 different species. Numerous commercial operators offer fishing trips – most have booths along the Esplanade in St Peter Port, or advertise at the ferry terminals on Alderney, Herm and Sark. For a comprehensive guide to island angling visit www.guernseyfishingguide.com.

Cycling

Visit Guernsey publishes an excellent guide to waymarked cycle paths on the island, called *Cycle Tours: 11 Island Routes*. For bicycle hire details, *see page 72.*

Toddler in tow

Walking

Endless walking possibilites

A programme of guided walks runs from April to September. Information is available from the Tourist Information Centre, which also provides a series of trail leaflets. The centre also has maps that enable visitors to follow the Victor Hugo Trail in St Peter Port. *(See also walks detailed on pages 40–3.)*

Golf

Guernsey has two 18-hole courses. The premiere is a links at L'Ancresse Royal Guernsey (tel: 01481 2476523); La Grande Mare is at Vazon Bay, Castel (tel: 01481 253544); there is also a nine-hole par three course designed by Tony Jacklin at St Pierre Park Hotel, St Peter Port, (tel: 01481 727039). Non-members and visitors are welcomed.

Watersports

For sailing or windsurfing lessons contact the Guernsey Sailing Trust (tel: 01481 710877; www.sailingtrust.org.gg) who run courses at all levels. The Guernsey Surf School at Vazon offers lessons and courses in surfing, along with kayak tours, coasteering, zorbing (rolling inside a giant transparent plastic ball) and catsailing (for information tel: 01481 244855; www.guernseysurfschool.co.uk). The Blue Dolphins Sub Aqua Club (tel: 01481 712492), a branch of the British Sub Aqua Club, caters for everyone, from beginners to experienced divers.

Young recruits at St Peter Port

Indoor sports

The Beau Séjour Leisure Centre, Amherst, St Peter Port (tel: 01481 726964 for sports bookings) is great for those rainy days. The main pool has water slides and play island facilities, and there is a smaller pool for toddlers. The leisure centre also offers roller skating, gym, squash, badminton, football, volleyball, tennis, a fitness studio, sauna and spa.

Getting There

By air

Opposite: traditional transport on Sark

UK visitors flying direct from the UK do not need a passport, but a passport or photo ID is compulsory, even for inter island flights, if you book on-line and have a paperless ticket. Prices can vary considerably but it is usually cheaper to book on-line direct with the airlines.

Flybe currently operates direct flights from London Gatwick, Birmingham, Exeter and Southampton plus indirect flights from Belfast, Edinburgh, Glasgow, Norwich and Manchester. For further information tel: 0871 700 2000; www.flybe.com. **Aurigny** operates direct flights from London Gatwick, London Stansted, Bristol, Manchester, Jersey, Alderney and Dinard. For further information tel: 0871 871 0717; www.aurigny.com. **Blue Islands** operates direct flights from Bournemouth, Southampton, Jersey and Alderney. For further information tel: 0845 620 2122 or visit www.blueislands.com. For private pilots there is the advantage of cheap fuel at Guernsey Airport; contact **Guernsey Aeroclub** (tel: 01481 265267; www.guernseyaeroclub.com).

At Guernsey airport, taxis are usually available (a cab to St Peter Port costs about £9) but it is advisable to book ahead. The largest operator is Delta (tel: 01481 200000). Buses run every 15 minutes at peak times. Most of the car hire firms *(see page 72)* meet passengers at the Airport.

Inter-island flight

By ferry

Condor Ferries (tel: 0845 609 1024; www.condorferries. com) runs a high-speed catamaran service from Weymouth all year round (2 hours 10 minutes) and from Poole May to September (2 hours 40 minutes). Ferries take cars as well as passengers. Bad weather conditions can lead to the cancellation of a crossing. Condor also operates a conventional ferry service from Portsmouth (13 hours). From Guernsey, it is a 20-minute ferry hop to Herm and 45 minutes to Sark; Jersey and Alderney are each a 15-minute flight away, or one hour by sea.

Condor craft

Getting Around

Public transport

Guernsey has a good network of scheduled bus services, all operating on a flat fare of 60p, Wave & Save smart cards for £1 save up to 60 percent on the individual flat fare. Most run at least once an hour and on some routes every 15 minutes. Timetables are accessible online at www. buses.gg. Bus stops are clearly marked on the road surface but outside St Peter Port you can 'hail' the bus. Multi-journey vouchers can be bought and most hotels supply timetables and route maps.

Rustic signposting

Several companies operate scheduled or tailor-made bus tours, including Island Coachways (tel: 01481 720210), Intransit (tel: 01481 700066) and Island Courier Services (tel: 01481 200001).

Taxis

The main taxi rank is opposite the Bankers Draft pub and Weighbridge roundabout, and other ranks are at the top of Smith Street and in Market Square. On Alderney, the main rank is in Victoria Street or you can phone ABC Taxis on 01481 823760 or J S Taxis on 07781 100830.

Car hire

With no VAT to pay, and low import duties, car hire on Guernsey ought to be cheap. In practice, costs are boosted by high insurance charges, though they are still cheaper than elsewhere in Europe. Child seats and cars with automatic transmission cost extra. Fuel is about 75 per cent of the UK price. Drivers must be over 20 and have held a full licence for a year. Car hire companies in Guernsey include Harlequin Hire Car (tel: 01481 239511; www.harlequinhire.com) and Hertz (tel: 01481 239516; www.hertzci.com). On Alderney, try Braye Hire cars (tel: 01481 823881) or Drive Island (tel: 01481 822971).

Alderney public transport

Bicycle hire

Cycle hire shops are plentiful on Alderney (by the harbour in Braye, and in Victoria Street) and on Sark (at the top of Harbour Hill and along the Avenue). On Guernsey, try Millards (tel: 01481 720777) or Guernsey Cycle Hire Company (tel: 07781 192033).

Ferry services

Herm: Travel Trident (tel: 01481 721379) operates 250-

seater catamarans from St Peter Port to Herm roughly every hour in high season. The booking office is on the corner of North Esplanade and St Julian's Pier.

Sark: The Isle of Sark Shipping Company (tel: 01481 724059) offers day trips to Sark, with add-on options of lunch, a two-hour carriage ride, and entry to the Seigneurie Gardens. The booking office is on St Julian's Pier.

Day trips to Jersey and France: Condor Ferries operates day trips from St Peter Port to Jersey, and to St-Malo. Manche Îles Express operates ferries connecting Guernsey with Jersey, and Carteret and Diélette in Normandy (both take 60 minutes; www.manche-iles-express.com).

Alderney: the best way to visit Alderney from Guernsey is to take the 15-minute flight operated by Aurigny or Blue Islands *(see page 71)*.

Bicycles are everywhere

Driving on Guernsey

Most roads are very narrow, visibility can be poor at junctions, and the lanes are used by tractors, cyclists, pedestrians and horses, as well as buses and cars. A maximum speed limit of 35mph (55kph) applies on all rural roads on Guernsey and Alderney; in towns it is 25mph (40kph).

A yellow line across the junction of a minor road means stop and give way to traffic on the major road. A yellow arrow on the road warns of a junction ahead. Many junctions on Guernsey have a filter-in-turn-system, marked by a cross-hatched yellow box painted on the road. You must not enter the box until your exit is clear.

A single yellow line along the side of the road means no parking at any time. On Guernsey and Alderney, all street parking is free, but in towns you must use a parking disk. Disks are supplied with hire cars or available from the Guernsey Visitor Centre in St Peter Port.

We recommend *Insight Fleximap: Channel Islands*, which is laminated for durability and ease of use.

The Herm ferry

73

Facts for the Visitor

Travel documents

Although a passport isn't necessary for visitors arriving from the UK, either your passport or photo ID is compulsory at check-in desks for travellers with paperless tickets.

Single-lane traffic

Tourist information

Guernsey Information Centre, North Esplanade, St Peter Port, Guernsey, Channel Islands, tel: 01481 723552; www.visitguernsey.com.

Herm Island, Herm, Channel Islands, tel: 01481 723552; www.herm-island.com.

Sark Visitors' Centre, The Avenue, Sark, Channel Islands, tel: 01481 832345; www.sark.info.

Alderney Information Centre, Victoria Street, St Anne, Alderney, tel: 01481 822811; www.visitalderney.com.

Sightseeing

Most attractions are free for young children and substantial reductions are given to senior citizens and students. The Guernsey Museums Service passport saver ticket allows discounted entry to its museums.

Money

Sterling is accepted on all the islands, as are UK cheques, credit cards and cash machine cards. Guernsey issues its own banknotes and coins, which can only be used in Guernsey, Jersey, Sark, Herm and Alderney (though UK banks will exchange Guernsey notes for sterling). Some banks have one ATM for sterling, one for local currency.

Postage

The Bailiwick of Guernsey issues its own postage stamps and you must use these for mail posted on the islands: UK stamps are not valid, and neither are Jersey stamps.

Telephones and Internet

Telephone kiosks operated by Cable & Wireless accept cash or phone cards, available at newsagents and many stores. Also available are reasonably priced Sims for unlocked mobile phones. Most mobiles work on the islands but some networks require a roaming facility plus international dialling code. Check with your provider.

The place for post

Guernsey, Herm, Sark and Alderney are within the UK telephone system, sharing the area code 01481. To call elsewhere in the UK, dial the area code and number. To call outside the UK, dial the international access code (00), country code, and area code, omitting the initial 0.

Internet access is available at the airport, the tourist office and the Guille-Alles library next to the market. Only a handful of hotels offer wi-fi internet access.

Local money

Time

The Channel Islands follow Greenwich Mean Time (GMT).

Opening times

Bank, shop and post office opening times are the same as those of the UK. Most museums and tourist attractions are open from 9am or 10am to 5pm from April to October, and some of the major sites are open all year.

Smoking

Smoking is not permitted in enclosed public areas in Guernsey and Herm. Sark does not have any legislation on smoking; Alderney is considering it.

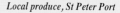

Local produce, St Peter Port

Public Holidays

These are the same as those of the UK with the addition of Liberation Day on 9 May.

Shopping

75

In theory, shopping in the Channel Islands ought to be cheap because there is no VAT to pay on purchases and because import duties are low. In reality, the cost of freighting goods to the Channel Islands sometimes cancel out the gains. People do come here to buy jewellery, cameras and electronic goods, but you need to do your homework before you arrive and have a good idea how much the same model would cost back home.

In St Peter Port, the leading British High Street retailers have their premises along the High Street, but there are also many small, attractive independent shops selling clothing, antiques, books, perfume and jewellery, especially in The Arcade and Le Pollet. Guernsey also has many craft centres, galleries and retail outlets dotted around the island, may of which are described in this guide.

Bargains by day, songs by night

Nightlife and entertainment

Get a monthly *Diary of Events* from Visit Guernsey *(see page 73)* or go to www.guernseytickets.gg. The *St James Diary* lists concerts, exhibitions, poetry readings and lectures hosted by St James, the church in College Street, St Peter Port, which now forms Guernsey's premier arts venue (www.stjames.gg). The Arts Council of Guernsey also publishes a free bi-monthly magazine, *Artefact*, which includes details of arts organisations, plus an events diary.

Guernsey has a four-screen cinema showing new releases, near the airport at the Mallard Hotel Cinema Complex, La Villiaze (tel: 01481 266366). Alderney has a small cinema on Victoria Street.

Folk entertainment

Choices in St Anne

Live Music: There are several pubs offering live music; among them are The Cock and Bull in Hauteville (tel: 01481 722660) and The Golden Lion in Market Street (tel: 01481 727711). A weekly live music listing is on http://gig guide.guernseyonline.com. During late July and early August, posters advertise concerts in the 'Valestock' series, an annual festival of rock and folk music, with open-air performances at Vale Castle, just north of St Sampson. In the same setting, the Vale Earth Fair, at the end of August, features local and international bands in Guernsey's own version of Glastonbury. The Doghouse, Rohais, St Peter Port (tel: 01481 721302; www.doghouse.gg) has live music most nights, plus monthly UK tribute bands. Currently it is the best venue in town for live entertainment, atmosphere and good food.

Medical care

Starting from 1 April 2009 visitors to the Bailiwick of Guernsey must pay for health services, so it is wise to take out medical insurance. Most visitors seeking treatment are suffering from sunburn. There is little or no light pollution in Guernsey, and people often seriously underestimate the strength of the sun, so make sure you pack a high-factor sun cream. Contact the following if you are in need of emergency medical care:

Guernsey: Pier Steps Surgery, High Street, St Peter Port (located in the basement of Boots), tel: 01481 711237; or any of the surgeries on the island.

Sark: The Medical Centre, Rue la Rade, Sark, tel: 01481 832045.

Herm: No medical facilities on the island, though residents can call up helicopter-borne emergency services if the situation is serious enough.

Alderney: The Island Medical Centre, Sundial House, Les Rocquettes, tel: 01481 822077.

Emergencies

In an emergency dial 999 or 112 for police, fire, ambulance or coastal rescue services.

Disabled access

Special parking areas are available for Blue Parking Card holders. Public conveniences for the disabled, fitted with radar locks, can be found in the main centres and at most of the beaches. For hire of equipment visit www.ambulance.org.gg/carehome.htm, or contact the tourist information offices.

Pets

Dogs and cats are now normally able to gain entry via the Pets Passport Scheme. Check with your chosen carrier.

Guernsey for Children

If you and your children are still young enough at heart to enjoy all the pleasures of the beach, then there is no better destination for a family holiday. Sea temperatures do not become comfortable for swimming until mid-July – but that coincides nicely with school summer holidays.

At cooler times of the year, paddling is still an option, and beachcombing is fun year round – the huge tidal flows that take place in the Channel Islands (there is between 20 and 25ft/6–8m difference between high and low water mark) mean that huge expanses of sand and crab-filled rock pools are revealed when the water goes out. Shell Beach, on Herm, is a famous spot for shell hunting.

For much of the year, Guernsey and the smaller islands enjoy a climate more akin to that of Northern France than southern England – but rain can be a problem in spring as fronts come in off the Atlantic. This is the time to head for the **Beau Séjour Leisure Centre** *(see page 69)*, on the hilltop above St Peter Port, to enjoy the swimming pool, with its flume slides and floating islands.

Other formal attractions in St Peter Port include the **Guernsey Museum** *(see page 25)*, which has friendly staff and activity sheets that will keep older children (eight-years-old and above) quiet for an hour or so; **Fort Grey** *(see page 29)*, which also has activity sheets focusing on the wrecks that have been found around Guernsey's shores; and **Castle Cornet** *(see page 19)*, which puts on organised activities for children during the summer, teaching them about life in an 18th-century garrison.

Two attractions, with confusingly similar names, are perfect for children: **Saumarez Park** *(see page 36)* has an adventure playground in the grounds, and the Folk Museum provides a fun introduction to the island's history

Top guns

Sculpture at Sausmarez Manor

– including the ancient practice of child labour. The tea rooms here are also very child friendly with freshly made and reasonably priced food. **Sausmarez Manor** *(see page 26)*, in a different part of the island, has pets, crazy golf and a number of other diversions for children. Apart from these, you will find plenty of other attractions, from the **Little Chapel** *(see page 31)* with its shell-encrusted walls, to **Oatlands Village** *(see page 38)* and the Aquarium in St Peter Port *(see page 22)*.

Going to Sark or Herm by boat is an adventure in itself, and the journey is short enough for children not to get bored. Once there, there are no cars to worry about, so children can roam in relative safety, and Sark can be enjoyed either by bike or by the more sedate horse and carriage – but don't forget sunscreen.

Accommodation

The States of Guernsey Tourist Board publishes a comprehensive illustrated guide to all the accommodation available on the islands of Guernsey, Herm, Sark and Alderney. It is available with a free DVD from Visit Guernsey, PO Box 23, St Peter Port, Guernsey, Channel Islands GY1 3AN (tel: 01481 723555). Information is also available on the internet at www.visitguernsey.com. The website also shows the latest tour operator specials. Tour companies specialising in Guernsey include Saga holidays (tel: 0800 414441; www.saga.co.uk/travel-shop), Premier Holidays (tel: 0844 493 7529; www.premierholidays.co.uk/guernsey) and Channel Islands' Travel Service (tel: 0845 470 1177; www.guernseytravel.com).

Hotels, self catering and camping

The selection below is listed according to the following categories: £££ (over £150 a night for a double room); ££ (£90–150 a night for a double room); £ (under £90 a night for a double room). Prices include breakfast.

Mille Fleurs, Guernsey

Guernsey

The Ambassador Hotel, Route de Sausmarez, St Martins, GY4 6SQ, tel: 01481 238356; www.ambassadorguernsey.co.uk. Small, reasonably priced, well run private hotel close to several beautiful bays. Heated swimming pool in mature gardens. Popular restaurant and bar. ££

Bella Luce Hotel, La Fosse, St Martin, GY4 6EB, tel: 01481 238764; www.bellalucehotel.com. Ancient manor house which underwent a transformation in 2008. Colonial-style decor, good food, swimming pool and popular '60s-style bar which has reopened after 36 years. Excellent value. ££

Côbo Bay Hotel, Côbo, Castel, GY5 7HB, tel: 01481 257102; www.cobobayhotel.com. Ideal beach holiday hotel opposite sandy Côbo Bay. Award-winning restaurant. Private complimentary health suite with day spa. ££

Fauxquets Valley Campsite, Castel, GY5 7QA, tel: 01481 255460; www.fauxquets.co.uk. Wonderful campsite in a tranquil valley. All amenities including heated pool, licensed restaurant and bar, shop and children's playground and games room. £

La Fregate Hotel, Les Cotils, St Peter Port, GY1 1UT, tel: 01481 724624; www.lafregatehotel.com. Stylish, deluxe boutique hotel in the centre of St Peter Port. Fantastic views across the islands and one of the best restaurants in Guernsey. £££

Hotel Bon Port, Moulin Huet Bay, St Martins, GY4 6EW, tel: 01481 239249; www.bonport.com. The only hotel to overlook the beautiful Moulin Huet Bay and famous 'Peastacks', which were immortalised by Renoir. Tasteful en-

Herm's White House Hotel